TWO YEARS BEHIND THE HELM
From the Office to the Ocean

∽

Cam Seamus

∽

A Cutwater Publishing Memoir

© 2019 Cam Seamus

Published in the United States, in the city of Murrieta, California
by Cutwater Publishing.

First Edition: 2021

Paperback ISBN 978-1-7362349-0-7
eBook ISBN 978-1-7362349-1-4
Library of Congress Catalog Number - 2021910894

Senior Editor - Morgan Bone
Developmental Editor - Theodore Niekras
Editor - Kimberly Albury
Editor - Laurie Taylor
Cover design by Fajar Wahyu

To learn more about the author and his other projects, visit:

https://cutwaterpublishing.com

This book is dedicated to all those who have influenced and supported my desire to sail oceans. Thank you.

CONTENTS

TWO YEARS BEHIND THE HELM
From the Office to the Ocean

∾

Cam Seamus

"Any purposeful movement in the universe ultimately involves an intention to proceed to a definite point, and navigation is the business of proceeding in such a manner as to arrive at that point."[1]

Dutton's Navigation and Piloting
-Hill, Utegaard, and Riordan

---

[1] Use by permission, United States Naval Institute, Annapolis Maryland

INTRODUCTION

Mine isn't a story of epic storms, pirates, shipwrecks, or the many other dramatic topics surrounding sea travel; it's the story of a life that was off-course - a life un-lived.

How is it that despite our best efforts we can end up so far from where we intended to go? Sailors know that even when aiming directly for something, they can end up somewhere else if the current is pushing them away from their intended destination. The sailing term for this is Set and Drift. Life works in much the same way. We begin with a goal in mind and then unplanned events occur: a job changes, a relationship ends, a child is born, a loved one dies. Life happens. A course is determined, and we are then affected by the current of life pushing us one way or another. We may become a piece of driftwood floating along with it, a drowning swimmer pulling hard against a rip current, a ship sailing proudly into a harbor on a following flood current. Set and Drift.

Of course, there are times when we drift because we never chose a destination. What do you want to be when you grow up? The question asked by adults when we're kids often follows us through our lives. How do you get somewhere if you don't know where you're going? One day you wake up, look around and wonder - *how the hell did I get here?*

Are you setting the right course in life and then steering accurately? There's a rule in navigation called the "1 in 60" rule which states: for every 1º we are off course, we will be 1 mile off course for every 60 miles traveled. What happens if we do this over and over in our lives? We arrive somewhere we never intended to go, or worse yet, never arrive at all. It's easy to miss an island in the middle of an ocean even if you are only 1º off course.

In my case it was a combination of all three things. Set and Drift, the wrong course, and faulty navigation. I ended up so far off course that despite all the indications of success, I was lost at sea.

One night, I found myself sitting in the dark, on a sailboat hundreds of miles from land, struggling with what to write in my journal. I desperately wanted to write something. I began to think about honesty, and I realized how critical it is on the ocean: Where are we? Where are we going? How long will it take? How much drinking water do we have? Lying to yourself or your crew can be a death sentence. Then again, how is that any different from our day-to-day lives on land? Any of the lies we tell ourselves can eventually become our undoing.

I wanted all of it to stop. To stop living in the false constructs of reality that I had created with my imagination to serve my ego. I wanted to be me – not some version of me I created to satisfy a corporate performance review. I wanted to be around people that accepted me – not people that constantly wanted me to be someone else. In the Pacific Ocean, hundreds of miles from shore, suddenly, reality hit me in the face. None of my lies and exaggerations matter out here – *the ocean is not impressed with me*. I sat humbled and in awe of nature. Suddenly, the dam of dishonesty cracked wide open and the ink began to flow from the pen.

PROLOGUE

"Those who fail to attend the motions of their own soul are necessarily unhappy." -Marcus Aurelius

For better or for worse, I walked away from a lucrative income with absolutely no idea of what was next. The only thing of which I was sure was that it was time to go – it was time to cast off my lines and leave the shore. I came to the obvious yet undeniable realization that life is short, and it must be lived. That was the day that I took an honest look at my life's checkbook and found it grossly overdrawn. I had failed to write the checks to pay for the important things – I had failed "to attend the motions" of my own soul.

Is the idea that we must work from graduation to grave nothing more than a system we have accepted? There is a promise offered to us of 'golden years' where we will play with grandchildren, look meaningfully into our partner's eyes, and reminisce about our life. It's what is sold to us on TV, by banks offering thirty-year mortgages, and financial planners with 401K retirement plans. Yet it's possible to spend so much of our life working that we allow life itself to pass us by, and therein lies the challenge. We live on borrowed time, accept a payment plan on our future, and have no assurance that tomorrow will ever arrive. Why are we willing to trade today for the hope of a better tomorrow?

I remember the days leading up to my departure, and how desperately I wanted something tangible in my life. For once, I wanted to work on something that would last longer than the next market cycle. By the time I came to the choice of stay or go, it felt like everything was intangible. I was stuck in a maze where the exit was constantly moved, feeling like the next left turn would lead me out, only to find another dead end. Exhausted from its endless churn, I finally realized that I wasn't living. Then I began to see that I had helped build the maze, and actually held the key to my own release.

Thoreau wrote in Walden: "The mass of men lead lives of quiet desperation, and go to the grave with the song still in them."

I realized that if I didn't change, the desperate life I was living would be my only legacy to my children. They saw this even more clearly than I did. They were the witnesses who could testify that I was working too much, letting stress take its toll, and that I never, ever stopped to watch the sunset. The spirit of our humanity was almost extinguished by the way I had chosen to "live" - there was only a small ember deep inside me that remained. It was time to stoke the fire.

MAYDAY, MAYDAY, MAYDAY

May 2018
Dearborn, Michigan

It had been an unusually cold winter, and spring had never arrived. The month of May wasn't much different; cold, gray, and wet. My mood mirrored the weather and there was no sunshine on my horizon. I had seen enough depression in family and friends to know the warning signs, and they were everywhere I looked. I was chronically exhausted, sleeping poorly, and having a hard time getting out of bed. Subsisting mostly on a diet of sarcasm, as if it was all I had left to ease the pain of the absurdity I felt all around me.

There were moments when I would think that I could outlast the feelings, somehow bootstrap my way through the next few years to retirement. I had come so far and sacrificed so much to climb the corporate ladder, and I was so close to the top. Part of me said, "I can't quit now." The Boston song *Peace of Mind* would run through my mind: climbing the proverbial corporate ladder and the purposelessness of the effort. Would they say at my funeral, "He was a hard worker," or "He answered more emails at 8:00 p.m. than anyone could ever imagine!" or even, "Can you believe he sacrificed so much time away from his family for the company?" No one cared. I was cultivating the most boring and pathetic eulogy possible. This wasn't living. It couldn't be. There had to be something more, something I was missing.

In contrast to my own life, I watched people on YouTube living the life of which I dreamt. Seeing them sail to palm tree covered islands with white sandy beaches inspired me. Most of them did not have great resources or vast experience, yet they were crossing oceans and exploring distant islands. I was contemplating the question, *How do I do that?* More importantly, I asked the question, *What's stopping me - is it just a decision I need to make?*

Two days before I resigned, I heard someone say, "We are in an extremely live, fluid, dynamic market." That phrase, which I will never forget, was one of the last pieces to drop into place. It helped me see the absurdity of all of it. You didn't work together and take everything into consideration, you collaborated holistically. You didn't get off track, you went down the rabbit hole. We had corporate code for almost everything: fifty-thousand-foot view, circle the wagons, stay out of the weeds, informed, North Star, here's the rub, boil the ocean, disrupt – the list went on and on. Meaningless phrases from the latest business book at the airport, which said essentially the same thing as the last book had said, but with new, made-up, catchy phrases. All flash, no substance. You couldn't just say what you meant, you had to say it in a certain way. Catch phrases would move the conversation in your direction if you said them in a certain tone. It was BS and I was sick of it. My soul was awakening to the importance of being honest with myself.

The next day, I called my wife Laurie and said, "I may quit tomorrow. I'm going to sleep on it, and I'll know in the morning." After nearly 30 years of being married to me, almost nothing surprised her.

She knew how unhappy I'd been. She said, "Okay, we'll figure it out. Do what you have to do."

On the morning of Friday, May 11, I wrote an email at home and saved it to my drafts file. The message was simple: I was resigning to do some sailing and writing, this was through no fault of the company, it was a personal decision. It would be impossible for me to explain in any detail beyond that, in some part because I didn't yet understand it myself. The twenty-minute drive to the office was my last time to think it over. It was both the longest and shortest twenty-minute drive I have ever taken.

Pulling into the parking lot of our company offices, I was confronted with the dullness of the world I had come to hate. Gray skies sat above gray clouds, which floated above gray concrete, surrounded by dead grass, barren trees, and asphalt. I went into my office. More gray, in the form of hideous, temporary cubicles.

It was gray outside, gray in my office, and gray in my life. Gray could easily describe 90% of the meetings, phone calls, and emails. I was tired of it and it had to change. I opened my laptop and sent the email to the President. My resignation after nearly eighteen years flashed over the corporate server to her inbox; I was done.

Mayday, Mayday, Mayday. The three words sailors only use when life or vessel is in jeopardy. I had made the call, as I was sinking. When a mariner calls a Mayday, anybody who is close will come to their aid. My closest friends in Michigan, my family, and the sailing community around the world rallied around me in support. I had made the call just in time – all was not lost.

One week later, I was crossing Lake Erie on a Catalina 30 with its mast lashed to the deck. Soon after that, I would sail the length of Lake

Huron, and part of Lake Michigan. My life was suddenly very different, and while the change was necessary and welcome, it was also jarring. But I needed that kind of sudden force to wake me from the slumber in which I had lived for so long. Within four weeks of my resignation, I completed a 100 Ton Captain's course, and saw more of Michigan than I had in the prior three years. It was a swift reminder of how much life I had let slip away.

I bought a new journal, it begged me to write on its pages. With all of the newfound time I had on my hands, I thought it would be easy. Instead, it was a desperate failure. For the next nine months, it would be nothing but fits and starts, torn out pages, and lined out paragraphs. The words coming out were not my own, there were those of others. Words I had read in a self-help book, words from a performance review, words from old creeds I had known, words of my parents. I had to find my own voice - I had no idea how long and arduous that journey would be.

THE OTHER SIDE
OF THE WORLD

July 2018
Corfu, Greece

Less than sixty days after leaving my career of nearly thirty-years, I stepped off the plane in Corfu, Greece, to sail a boat. It was surreal. It was hard to believe that I was halfway around the world and going to work on a boat. My original plan had been to take my own thirty-two-foot sailboat, *Trillium*, from the Great Lakes through the Erie Canal, and out to the Atlantic. However, while I was ready to sail away, my boat wasn't. It quickly became apparent that *Trillium* was going to need a major refit before any long passages.

With *Trillium* in the boat yard, I explored the possibility to do something I hadn't yet considered. Rather than sailing my own boat on a long journey, I could join a crew on someone else's boat. This idea seemed to make sense for a lot of reasons. First, it allowed me to get on the water fast – which is where I desperately needed to be. Second, as an extrovert, I would probably be happier as part of a crew, rather than being a solo-sailor. I was also realizing that sometimes you need to run in the direction of the wind instead of fighting against it. This invisible wind was leading me on a different journey, one that I had not envisioned.

I joined an online crew sharing site and found a sailboat in Greece that needed a crew member. It was such a long shot that I almost didn't apply for the position; after all, the Mediterranean was full of people who were far more qualified than I was at the time. But there was something about the way that the owner had written the posting that gave me the sense that he would understand my journey, that he would be willing to help. I sent the application not expecting to hear anything back and was shocked to find a reply in my inbox a few days later. After a few more emails and phone calls, I was welcomed to the crew. I could hardly believe it myself when I shared the news with my family and friends.

The heat in Corfu was sweltering as I walked down the stairs from the plane onto the hot tarmac, and then toward the small terminal that probably dated back to 1960. It was run down and worn out, just like me. I wondered if it would be ever restored. I wondered if I ever could be.

As I walked along, I began to consider the ways that this journey was changing me. There were the barriers that I had to break down that lived in the realm of control, fear, and ego. It was hard to relinquish control of so many things in my life, such as my career, and my "plan." Control gives us a sense of comfort as we blindly believe that our span of influence is far greater than it actually is. Fear manifests itself in many ways, sometimes as control, sometimes as ego. I had to let go of imaginary threats to my safety and future if I was to take this journey and stop worrying about what other people think.

But, fear and ego sought to dissuade me, as they had so many times over the years. This wasn't what I told people I was going to do; I had said I was going to sail my own boat from the Great Lakes to the Caribbean. *What will people think?* They may see it as evidence of my failure. Questions began to pollute my mind; *Can I control their perception? What if the captain is not there when I arrive? What if it's a scam? What am I getting myself into?* I fought against these inner demons with all my heart, threw caution to the wind, and kept walking forward. It was one of the best decisions of my life.

After entering the old terminal at the Corfu Airport, I made my way to the customs line for non-EU visitors. Listening to an unfamiliar mix of languages and accents in the line around me: British, Greek, German; trying to pick up on familiar words, something that might remind me of home. The dank air created a tension that clouded my mind. Another imagined fear crept up on me; the customs agent would interrogate me. The fifteen-minute wait, the humidity, and the oppressive heat worked together to heighten my anxiety. I had watched too many spy thrillers where the plot twist occurred in the customs line. As my turn to clear customs drew closer, my heart rate increased. When I finally stood in front of the heavyset, darkly tanned man, he looked up with an air of boredom, and in heavily accented Greek, simply said, "Passport." They didn't seem to care who I was, why I was there, or when, if ever, I was leaving. If they had asked, how could I begin to explain to him or anyone what I was doing there? I barely understood myself – maybe that's what really scared me.

Walking outside, I hailed a cab. "Gouvia Marina," I said as I threw my backpack on the back seat and slid in next to it. We sped through tiny streets in a big Mercedes and wound our way to the marina.

Discovering that taxi aroma is universal, even in idyllic Greece, I cracked a window. The driver lit a cigarette, and carelessly sped along, concentrating more on the radio than the road. I had been traveling for almost twenty-four hours and I was exhausted. I closed my weary eyes and contemplated my fate in the hands of the taxi driver. *Have I flown to another continent to be killed in a traffic accident?* I smiled and rolled the window down further. If I survived the ride, all I wanted at that point in life was a meal, a shower, and a bed, preferably in that order. I asked the driver how to say thank you in Greek. "Efcharistó," he answered in a coarse, husky voice, courtesy of the cigarettes on the dashboard.

Observing the town as we raced along, I could see influences of its French Colonial past. Once proud and now dilapidated buildings, deteriorating beneath hideous billboards advertising expensive fur coats. Trash was piled up in the streets as Greece had never fully recovered from its own economic crisis. The juxtaposition of extreme poverty and extreme wealth was jarring. *What the hell am I doing here?* It was the only question I could find as I tried to process all of what I was seeing and feeling.

Leaning back in the seat of the cab, I began to answer my own question. *Maybe here, I will be far enough away from there. Maybe here, I can be honest with myself. Maybe here, I can just be myself.* I was beginning to understand that the chart which had led me to the breaking point was littered with reefs of self-dishonesty. Some of those reefs arose from my own failure to be myself.

NEW HORIZONS

July 2018

Gouvia Marina, Corfu, Greece

The taxi dropped me off inside the marina next to the stores and restaurants. Before taking in my surroundings, I called the owner of the boat, and let him know I had arrived. In his heavily accented English, the Dutchman said he would be along shortly, and told me where to wait for him

Making my way down to the edge of the docks, I examined the boats in the massive marina and all of the activity surrounding them. As much as I loved sailing and the sea, it had never occurred to me that this could have been a career choice many years ago. I saw uniformed crew heading out to super-yachts and then it dawned on me; I was now one of the nameless and faceless crew members that came and went from marinas all over the world. It was hard to believe. At fifty-four years old, nothing more than determination had helped me crack the code to become a member of this elite group.

I was certainly well-qualified in most respects: I had been sailing for over thirty-five years and I had completed the training for my captain's license. On *New Horizons,* I would serve as a crew member without formal rank – which means you basically do whatever needs to be done, including the dishes. Looking around at these professional mariners, I envied all of them: the captains, cooks, stews, and deckhands. I envied them because they were living life on a set of terms I had never realized was possible. I had spent far too long living it on the terms of others.

There was a long concrete quay that ran southwest to northeast and sat five feet above the water. Its large, well-worn iron rings told the stories of past ships that had tied up, long before floating pontoon docks and plastic boats filled the marina. From the quay to the furthest dock on the end, it was just under a quarter mile walk. It was huge. I could see the mega yachts moored at the outer edges of the marina, their outlines towering above the smaller boats.

About ten minutes later, I saw a dinghy approaching the quay, driven by a man that looked like Fred from his online picture. He was accompanied by a young boy. Fred spotted me right away and gave me a wave. Walking briskly over to the quay to take their bowline I smiled and said, "Fred?" In his focused and energetic manner, he answered, "Hello, Cam. This is my son. Can you take this bag of trash?" I replied without hesitation, "Sure thing." That's the nature of yachtsmen, when there is a job to do, proper etiquette calls for lending a hand. He then added, "My other son is working on the boat. The boys will be with us for about a week." For some reason, the idea that his sons were there made me feel at home, like I was joining their family, and that's how Fred treated me from the start – like family.

Fred was tall and thin, his hair was cut close to his skull, and a few tattoos showed near his T-shirt sleeve hem. He was tan, and his face had an intensity that seemed to contradict the peace in his life that I would later come to understand. Somehow, this man who had pressed hard in his life and career and attained what many of us would have considered success, walked away from it and learned how to relax. He had risked everything on this new venture. His courage inspired me. Had some invisible force brought me to this place to learn from this man? It seemed more plausible with each moment. There is an old saying that goes, "When the student is ready, the teacher will appear." There are always lessons to be learned all around us, but we are not always ready to learn. In my case, it took a massive life change, and a flight halfway around the world to find my first teacher.

After I had thrown away the garbage in the nearby dumpster, I returned to the boat to find that they had already loaded my bag and were waiting to go with the engine still running. I eased my way carefully down the side of the steep concrete quay and into the small dinghy for the first of what would be many times in the next forty days. Fred navigated us out of the marina, and once we were past the five mile per hour zone, he accelerated. The bow of the dinghy pulled up out of the water as we headed out the channel. I felt the cool spray of the water from the bow wake on my face as my eyes took in the hillsides of Corfu. An old, white Greek Orthodox church stood out on the far shore of the inlet. I could feel the sun-drenched countryside already taking me by the hand, leading me somewhere important.

"There is a shallow area over there," he said loudly above the roar of the motor as he motioned toward it with his hand. "You'll want to avoid that area and stick close to the channel if you come over in the dinghy." As we came around the corner of the inlet, he motioned out over the bow and said, "There is *New Horizons*," as we raced toward the eighty-four foot yacht. She was just as beautiful in real life as she was in the photos. The boat was painted above the waterline in a rich navy-blue color, with well-maintained woodwork shining above the deck. She was waiting to receive me, to tell me her stories and listen to mine. There was no pretense, no judgement, and few expectations. This would be my first honest relationship in a very long time.

We boarded by means of a gangplank known as a passerelle, then made our way up and onto the boat. "Your quarters are up in the bow," Fred said as I followed him forward. "Why don't you get settled in, and then I'll show you around a bit later." Then, he added, "You must be tired, perhaps you would like to rest before dinner?" I agreed without hesitation, following him down into the quarters through the forwardmost hatch and climbing the few steps down an iron rung ladder. Fred continued, "Feel free to put up any pictures, or anything to make you feel at home." He smiled warmly. After showing me the location of switches, valves, and bedding that made up my quarters, he said, "Okay, we'll see you later." I replied, "What time do you want me up for dinner?" He smiled again, and said, "When you are ready." Fred, it became apparent, was one of the warmest and most genuine people I would ever meet. Regardless of our beliefs, it seems hard to deny that when we are open, the right people often appear in our life with the lessons we need to learn. That night, we sat on the back deck of *New Horizons* and talked about life. Like me, Fred had led a successful life in business and ended up feeling that he needed to take a different path, that of a sailor. Here I was, in Greece, talking to someone that had experienced everything that I had experienced. Was it coincidence? Sometimes it feels like I'm part of something larger than me; I seem to end up in the right places with the right people.

A shower helped to refresh and cool me off. With my body clean, my mind attempted to work on my situation as I sunk down into the bunk to rest. Exhausted, in a foreign land, separated from friends and family, struggling against stifling heat, I felt at home and at peace. I stopped fighting and fell deeply asleep. Since the day I had resigned, my sleep had become more peaceful, and my dreams more colorful. It was as if the cold and gray world that was so despised had been choking my imagination. Now, it churned while my soul rested quietly.

PARADISE FOUND?

July 2018
Paxos, Greece

It would be nice to think that when we leave a place, we leave our problems and unwanted emotions behind us; but it just isn't the case. There I was, halfway around the world, and I was about to face the same emotions and habits that had beset me back home: control, frustration, and a tendency to self-destruct. I didn't yet understand where it all originated, nor how I would ever stop the cycle.

A few days after arriving, we had sailed across the channel from the mainland of Greece and were planning on anchoring at Lakka, a small inlet at the northern end of Paxos Island. It was mid-afternoon and it had been another hot, windless day. As we came between the islands of Corfu and Paxos, the wind started to build. We hauled the sails up and turned off the motor. We were excited to finally be under sail, between two Greek Islands, on a sunny summer day. The warm wind and the blue waters of the Ionian Sea could have wrapped the eighty-four foot sailboat into a travel brochure for Greece that read, "Life is perfect here, come see for yourself."

We hadn't had the sails up for very long when it became apparent the wind and swell were building quickly. The forecast had been wrong.

"We need to drop our sails and head into Lakka for the night," I said, as we watched the situation changing from the interior of the boat's pilot house. Fred responded, "The guests want to sail out into the channel, why don't we reduce our sails and see how it goes?" It was a reasonable compromise, but since it wasn't *my* idea, it didn't sit well with me. This was a lesson that I needed to learn - there are often many versions of "right." Something about the turbulence of my upbringing made me feel the need for certainty, and that often translated into *very* firm opinions (to say the least).

New Horizons was a heavy displacement boat, a full keel ran from bow to stern along her eighty-four feet, weighing in at sixty-three tons. Her solid wood construction was certainly big and sturdy enough to handle some chop, but she wasn't built for Class A ocean sailing and we would pay attention to her limits as we watched the conditions building. It's amazing to watch how effortlessly the sea tosses around sixty-three tons. Over the course of the next few years, it would be the understanding and respect of this natural force of life and destruction that would finally set me free. But this was only the beginning of that journey, and I still had much to learn. Fred was an experienced skipper and he was well aware of the yacht's limitations. I should have trusted his experience, but I had an ego-driven need to be right. I wish I could say this was the first time in my life that I had overamplified a situation; that would be a lie. How is it that our perspective seems so clear as it plays out in our mind? I guess at some point, we are faced with a choice; *everyone else is wrong, or I am wrong.*

The swells in the Mediterranean are notably different from open ocean swells; closely spaced, they will prevent the boat from gliding up, over, and down into the next trough. Instead, depending on your angle, they can slam against the beam (side) of the boat, or slam the bow into the next wave. We were taking the waves at about a forty-five degree angle to the bow, so we were mostly slamming into the peak of the oncoming wave. It was turning into a roller coaster, and I continued the slow burn inside. I asked the parents to have the kids put on life jackets and bring them inside the boat, while Fred evaluated the sail plan.

Fred is a kind and gentle man that seeks, in his words, "open and honest" communication. On the other hand, I was like the neighborhood dog that takes off running once the door is opened. Fred was about to open the front door. "We will try to shorten the sail and stay out for a while," Fred began, and then with finality said, "This is the decision." His boat, his rules. There is no room for argument or dissent on a boat - the captain makes the call and the crew carries out the orders. I held my tongue and took the helm as he went forward to roll in the front sail. It wasn't a bad decision, but it bothered me because it wasn't what *I* thought we should do. "This is just going to keep building!" I yelled over the din of the wind, rigging and sea as he walked forward. "We need to get into that goddamn bay!" He looked at me in a puzzled fashion that conveyed: *Why are you speaking to me this way?*

The rolling device, called a furler, had been giving us some problems which turned this normally simple task into a Herculean one. I fired up the big diesel engine and held the big boat steady into the rolling swells and wind to keep the pressure off the sail, while Fred attempted to roll the massive canvas in. I watched with impatient intensity as he wrestled with the headsail. The massive lines, called sheets, that ran from the sail all the way back along the sides of the vessel to enormous drum winches, were snapping violently like a cowboy's whip. A hard lash to the head with one of those was certainly enough to knock someone out. When the sail was a little over halfway the progress just stopped. "What the hell is going on?" I wondered out loud to myself. Then Fred popped up and headed back toward me at the helm. "It's jammed – I can't fix it out here; we need to go in," as he motioned toward the bay. "No shit," I replied in a juvenile 'I told ya so' manner. Then, another outburst. "If this is how you're going to run the boat, I'm not staying on." He looked shocked and must have wondered what was going on with me because I had just overreacted to the situation. I still had mountains of garbage to sort through inside me. Years of holding back my voice for fear of a comment turning up on a performance review, or saying something in the wrong tone, or without a smile had left it all bottled up inside me. A tight lid on a jar under a lot of pressure had finally been opened. All of that kept spilling out onto others - which was no way to live. He replied, visibly hurt by my statement, "Okay, I'll drop you off at Corfu in a few days."

Leaving is a simple way of avoiding yourself. If I leave, it's because of what you did. If I leave, I don't have to face how I reacted. It's a coward's exit. If I leave, there is no chance of me failing. I wonder how many things I walked away from because I was afraid of failing? What did I walk away from because I was afraid of succeeding? I had a lot to sort out in my mind.

I wish I could blame that outburst solely on the years of biting my tongue during corporate meetings, but that would be a cop-out. In the end, whatever I did was all my own doing. If it was a result of biting my tongue all those years, it was after all *I*, who was biting *my* tongue. Responsibility still laid with me - not Fred; not the situation.

Later, as I reflected back on that day many times, I wondered, "What was I so mad about?" I was mad at myself. Mad that I had let so many years slip away. Furious that I had allowed others to take advantage of my kindness. Angry that I had worked so hard to succeed and while doing so, traded off pieces of myself. Going through life unaware that I had held so much in for so long, denying my own feelings. It surfaced like a Mediterranean storm – swift, strong, and from out of the blue. All of my past was directed at Fred in that moment. Fortunately for me, Fred had a big heart and open mind.

We got the boat into the bay at Lakka, with the partially furled headsail flogging about in the wind, vainly attempting to maintain our dignity as we looked for a spot to anchor among the multimillion-dollar super yachts. My mouth was dry, a sure sign of the adrenaline dump I had experienced thirty minutes earlier. I went about my after-anchor chores as I began to contemplate my reaction to the moment.

Once at anchor, Fred slid out onto the bowsprit with a few tools in hand, and within the hour he had the furler fixed and we settled in for the night like nothing had happened. Before we began the preparations for dinner, we started joking around to reduce the tension that I had needlessly caused. The wind had blown hard that day; hard enough from the north to jam the furling unit, and hard enough from my soul to damage my fledgling friendship with Fred. I was beginning to realize that I had a lot of work to do on myself, more than I had realized while dragging myself through days of endless meetings, when my faculties were focused on more "important" matters than my own soul. *Priorities Misplaced* could have been the tagline underneath my email signature. Even if it had been that obvious, I had been too blind to notice.

I didn't get off the boat. Instead, I chose a path that would force me to face my emotions. I apologized and started to open up to Fred – sometimes in ridiculous outbursts, other times by sharing something very personal. It would become a lasting perfect/imperfect friendship, as all real friendships are. He was the poor soul that the universe had put in my path to help me learn why it was so important to be open and honest; to learn that it wouldn't end well to hold in my true feelings indefinitely; to learn that they didn't need to arrive like storms.

It would take months for the sea to break down these embattlements inside of me, because I was still lying to myself and others to protect my ego. I still didn't understand why.

WHO AM I?

July 2018
Off the coast of Southern Italy

As the days passed under the sun that made the olives grow on the Greek hills, and my skin so deeply brown, I dropped a few pounds while becoming stronger and more flexible. My body, mind, and spirit were starting to recover. By this point in my life, I had endured disc injuries in my back and neck, as well as having both of my hips replaced. Seventeen years in a sedentary job had only exacerbated the genetic foundation provided to me in this life. Only a few weeks earlier, daily tasks on *New Horizons* had required more effort. I had struggled to climb around the lower rigging, move up and down the ladder to my berth and hop on and off the dinghy. Every move had felt like a struggle. Within three weeks, I found myself moving more quickly and with less effort. The boat was acting like a personal trainer, forcing me to do things out of the ordinary. Forcing me to move.

Most days would begin by hauling up buckets of sea water hand over hand from the deck which sat eight feet above the water. Haul a bucket, dump it onto the deck to wash it down. Over and over for the length of the deck on both sides of the eighty-four-foot boat. The task would work my arms, shoulders, back, legs, and heart. Many days would include a long swim in the salty, crystal clear water, and whenever I could get ashore, the longest walks I had ever taken in my life. My body was starting to recover from a life built around a desk and a chair. I was rested, eating a healthy diet, exercising daily, and adapting to my new world. On the outside things were changing faster than they were on the inside. That work still seemed like an abstract oil painting that had just been started. No pattern, no clear end in sight.

The days under the sun and sails, and the nights under crystal clear, starry skies were stimulating senses that had been dulled by the gray, concrete, and cubicle-bound life I had left behind. The small hardships I endured, such as heat and mosquitos, started to peel away the decades of softness I had developed in a well-manicured life. I had not always been that way; I had not always cared about comfort or ease. My youth was spent seeking rugged adventure in the mountains and I had fallen a long way from their peaks. The austere nature of boat life helped to purify my soul of the toxic cocktail distilled over decades.

I was growing weary of the stories that I told myself and others, stories built on some partial truths, exaggerated to cast me in a different light. These were nothing more than false constructs of reality which my imagination had built to serve my ego. For so long, my identity had been wrapped up in what I did, not who I was, and now I felt like a rudderless ship when someone asked me, "What do you do?" I finally just started saying, "I sail." I figured that was good enough for the time being.

One day, an idea came to my mind. In my journal I wrote the simple words: *I am.* I wanted to think about who I am, rather than what I do. What defines me as a person, what seems to be real in my life? It was more difficult than I imagined. We are so used to saying,

I'm a manager" or "I'm a student" or "I'm a (fill in the blank)." These words describe what we do, not who we are. What words would describe who I am? How often do we stop to consider *who we are?* It's difficult to evaluate ourselves honestly; sometimes we are too hard on ourselves, other times we self-soothe and delude.

I wrote out a list of things that seemed to come naturally to me, including, "I am watchful of others." Throughout my life, it has been something that I have done without thinking. I've witnessed a man and a woman in a heated argument that looked like it might get physical, and I have stepped in. Seeing kids playing on a dangerous stretch of beach who were then swept into the water, I have jumped in the water. It's a protective quality that keeps me on watch, wherever I go, whatever I do. It's part of *who I am*. After a few days, a list of characteristics lay before me. It was a revealing exercise that helped me begin to understand who I was: qualities that always seemed to orbit the gravity of my soul. I am a teacher, I am a protector, I am of the sea.

Throughout our lives, we are evaluated by what we do. Do your chores, get praise and an allowance. Do well in school, get a good grade. Do good work, get raises and positive performance evaluations. What you do, not who you are – this is what our society cares about, this is what rewards are based upon. Your closest friends and your family, these are people that care about *who* you are. It makes sense that for a society to operate, it must have merits (and punishments), for what we do. Unfortunately, as we can all attest, these merits are not meted out fairly. Many of the good things we do go unnoticed and unrewarded. We are rarely, if ever, acknowledged and appreciated for who we are on the inside.

After a lifetime of continuous grades and evaluations to prove my worth to others and society, suddenly, there was no one judging my every word and deed. I had at times been a straight "F" student, a straight "A" student, a U.S. Marine with high marks for proficiency and conduct, and meritorious promotions. I had worked in various companies being regularly given raises and promotions along the way - but always with the constant prodding to be something different than I was. *Nod your head in meetings so people know you are listening, smile when you walk to the bathroom so you don't stress people out* (yeah, someone actually said that to me), on, and on it went - never good enough. The performance review system had been designed so you did not, and could not, get an "A". The cheese kept moving.

In the Greek Islands, I was no longer facing the insane corporate scrutiny which measured the tone of my voice, every expression on my face, every word uttered, and every nuance of my personality. On *New Horizons*, I would never hear, "One thing you might want to work on..." On *New Horizons*, if I didn't meet expectations on the boat, they would just drop me off at the next port – a straightforward system, one with which I was quite comfortable.

At one point during the last year, I had written these words in my journal: "How long can you continue to be someone that you are not, until you are no one at all?" The question haunted me, for I had become aware in the year leading up to my departure that I was playing a role. I feared there was an invisible line I might cross, leaving me unable to ever find myself. Perhaps I had already gone too far. Had my whole life merely been a series of different facades? I had played so many roles, so which one was really me? Beach bum, straight "F" student, straight "A" student, US Marine, "Corporate Cam," singer/

songwriter, wandering sailor, professional mariner... who was I? Was I one of these things or all of them? These questions haunted me as I sailed, swam, walked, and dreamed that summer in the Mediterranean.

Most importantly, I was learning that it mattered not how others defined me, it mattered only how I defined myself. For me, that journey would be forged by the ocean - it was as if my life required such change that it could only be wrought by the power of the sea. The sea did not let me down.

ONE NIGHT IN TROPEA

July 2018
Off the coast of Southern Italy

After a short sail up Italy's southern coast, we anchored off Tropea, an ancient city on the west coast of the Calabria region. It was our second night out of Sicily and I was falling in love with Italy. The warmth of its land and people was a respite for my wandering soul. Our journey took us far south of the tourist destinations, right to the heart of where working families vacationed. There was nothing flashy about any of it; it was everyday life in Southern Italy, and its irresistible simplicity somehow reached inside of me and grabbed me with such a force, that I dream of retiring there to this day.

We arrived in the late afternoon and found a good anchorage just north of the town's harbor. Once the affairs of the boat were settled, I decided to take a short nap on deck in preparation for the evening's activities. My search for a spot to nap led me to the foredeck, where the huge jib (one of the front sails) was stowed along the rail. I nestled myself into the jib, using it as a bed and pillow, and dozed off while *New Horizons* sang me her songs through the rigging and wooden hull: *ting, creak, splash,* as the boat rolled gently. The song would carry on with a verse and then change to a chorus when something interrupted the rhythm: *creak, ting, creak.* My dreams were orchestrated by the sounds of the boat while Morpheus, the Greek god of dreams, conducted the symphony. I was resting peacefully.

I had been spending a lot of my free time resting. I was coming off a thirty-year stretch of push, push, push, that had led me to complete exhaustion. "Vacations" which I had taken in the past, were marred by the interruptions appearing on my so-called "smart" phone. Instead of sipping coffee overlooking the Pacific Ocean from my hotel room in Kona, I would catch up on email before my wife woke up. Throughout the day, I was distracted by emails, texts, and calls while I was supposed to be rejuvenating; a price I had been willing to pay to be "important" and to cash a big paycheck. So in some ways, that *was* the first time in thirty years I had completely stopped working. My exhausted mind and body screamed *carpe diem!* then immediately fell fast asleep.

Later on, I heard voices recalling me from my slumbering symphony. "Cam, where are you?" One of the boys called out in a heavy Dutch accent. Then I heard Julie's voice, "Here he is," in a Swedish accent. I was being prodded awake by our pirate crew. They proceeded to insist it was imperative that I join them in the evening's shore party. Although I felt exhausted and ancient in contrast to their youthful energy, I sleepily agreed to go into town with them. At the minimum, there was a thirty-year age spread between us. They treated me like the teenager I felt like underneath the exhaustion. As far as we were concerned, we were pirates about to storm the town. We hatched our plans, then waited for the best time to go forth, which certainly couldn't be earlier than 9:00 p.m. It was, after all, Italy.

Once the hour of departure had arrived, we said our goodbyes to Fred, who was kind enough to watch the boat while us "kids" went out to play. He gave us the requisite parental speech on being careful, and trusted me to ensure his boys, his guest, and his crew would be brought back safely. We spilled off the boat and into the dinghy like eager ants into sugar, while the engine fitfully sputtered. The gang liked to joke as I stepped on the dinghy, because my weight would cause it to sink so much into the water. After their good laugh at my expense, a bill I was more than happy to pay, we sped toward the harbor.

We found a suitable place to tie up the dinghy and I taught the kids the value of ten bucks. I showed the boys how to fold the bill so it fit in the palm of your hand, and then called the security guard over. "English?" I asked. "Sí, aaahh, yes," he replied. I went to shake his hand and pass him the money, while saying in my best mafioso voice, "You'll keep an eye on our dinghy for us, yes?" He hesitated only briefly as he felt the paper money press into his hand, and then eagerly agreed.

We walked the quarter mile or so along the concrete quay, with its endless line of multi-million dollar yachts backed up to it, laughing and joking about which one we would commandeer after we had plundered the town to our satisfaction. The marina had a shuttle service that ran every fifteen minutes, so while waiting, we talked about our priorities: food, drink, and music. After a short wait, all five of us, along with a British couple, and two locals – nine in total – piled into a van that seated seven. What could possibly go wrong? Seatbelts certainly weren't important on the steep, narrow, road from the marina to the town. After a few stops, we were dropped off and started to wander and argue some more about what we were actually looking for. After walking a few blocks, we planted ourselves like locals at a bar on a side street that was so old, it was hard for me to fathom. Huge stone blocks formed the surface of the street, and old buildings towered up several stories above them.

After our first round of drinks, the band took a break, and I asked if I could play a song or two while they were offstage. Having spent my life on stages, there was no longer any nervous energy or fear when I stood in front of a mic; it was just another part of who I am – a musician. The music, much like sailing, just seems to be inside me and sometimes I need to let it out. The crowd got quiet as the signature opening chords to *Free Fallin'* echoed down the cobblestone streets and against the ancient walls of this city. I wondered if these streets had ever heard Tom Petty before. I looked around at the audience and saw that I was connecting with them. A few patrons sang along while they heard my soul declare that I was in a free fall. If it's possible for a moment in time to merge a song and a heart, that was it. There was no sense of obligation to anything, no soul-crushing responsibility, no one demanding more of me. The city, the people, the crew, they took me as I stood before them, a wandering minstrel, who felt like he was falling through space and time to find his soul.

The manager came over and asked if I would continue to fill in for the band between sets, to which I gladly agreed. It had been a few months since I had played, and it felt good. We drank, ate, laughed, and lingered without a sense of time until we were ready to leave. Each moment folded effortlessly into the next as we ate fresh croissants at midnight, then fresh pizza, until we finally piled into another taxi and headed back to our dinghy and its privately guarded parking spot.

In many ways, the night in Tropea was more than just a night on the town. It was the embodiment of how I should have spent more time in the past, and how I will spend more time in the future. Free. Free to wander, free to laugh. To share my adolescent antics with anyone who will tolerate them. To let the song in my heart be heard, singing to the point of laughter and tears. One night in Tropea became a night to remind me what I was fighting for. A night to remember for the rest of my life. The memory would stand watch over me, vigilantly reminding me to live my life.

BACK ON LAND

August, 2018
Stabia, Italy

After forty days on *New Horizons*, I was ready to move on. My time there had been both difficult and easy, a contrast that would color the rest of the summer. Difficult, because I was feeling and expressing things honestly for the first time in my life. Easy, because I was unfettered and free to wander. Leaving the boat was both difficult and easy as well. Difficult, because I would miss the crew desperately, and I knew that this was a junction in the path. Easy, because I was ready for a real shower and some air conditioning.

New Horizons was tied 'stern to' in the Mediterranean fashion, with the back of the boat up against the concrete quay. I threw my backpack over my shoulder and made my way across the passerelle. The crew all lined up on the dock to say goodbye. A few of us, close to tears, assured each other we would stay in touch as we wished each other well. Each of them had received me without prejudice or judgement. They forgave my sins, which I assure you, were many. They accepted me for who I was on each day, as I unraveled, recomposed myself, and then unraveled again. A group of people let me be myself, even as I struggled to figure out who I really was: the epitome of true friendship.

I made my way through the gritty port city to the nearest ATM, and from there, it was a short walk to the train station. Stabia held none of the allure of the postcard versions of an old city in Italy; it was all function, and no form. Tall concrete buildings lined the streets, and grates rolled up from over storefronts that housed the small businesses as the city started to come to life.

I waited with patience at the train station on the northbound track for the train to Naples. Patience, a quality which for most of my life had eluded me, was now my contented companion. Life on the boat, in its own cadence and rhythm, had succeeded where parents, friends, books, and my spouse had failed – I was learning patience. There seemed to be a direct relationship between patience and anger, like a crime duo that worked together, robbing me of the simplest joys in life. I was no longer trying to punch through the atmosphere. I simply desired to breathe in the air around me.

Once on the train, I had no desire to read or write, despite the journal laying on the fold-out table. I wanted to think. After more than a month on *New Horizons*, there was still so much to consider. Who had I been all those years? What would I become now? How far would I still have to travel on this journey before any of it made sense? I guess you could describe some of it as post-traumatic stress. The train would rattle, jerk and then click-clack on the tracks. Italian and English filled the air as families and friends conversed. Staring out the window as the towns and cities passed along the train tracks gave me a perspective I hadn't seen from the coast. The cities were worn down, and tired – just like me. I wondered how they had become so run down, and if it was possible to resurrect them to their former glory. Then that haunting question again: Could I be resurrected?

In Naples, I changed trains for the trip to Rome. The station felt like a combination mall/airport with signs advertising the competing train companies, merchants selling food, and digital displays with train schedules above the boarding platforms. I made my way through the massive labyrinth of tracks and platforms, which looked like an anthill with people moving in all directions with single-minded purpose. A kind police officer helped me locate the correct platform, where I found a small convenience store to buy some snacks for the ride.

Once on board, I folded back into the seat of the high-speed train. Despite having rested for over two months, I was still tired. The rhythm of the train, the rhythm of life, and the rhythm of my soul seemed to coalesce as I lost myself in the journey. For thirty years, I maintained an intense focus in my life and career that had left me totally exhausted. As a result, I sat on a train in Italy with a desperate need to do absolutely nothing, to be absolutely no one, while the beautiful Italian countryside rolled by my window. Perhaps there is a villa in that town where I could just disappear for a year, I mused. This thought revealed my fear that I needed more time, but how much more?

My mind drifted back to *New Horizons*. What were my favorite memories? Was it my first night in Paxos, where I sat alone for hours and just watched people? Perhaps it was listening to the children play in the street, marveling at the centuries old fishing town, hearing all the different languages, and seeing so many things as if for the first time. Maybe it was all of the colors, textures, sounds, and smells I experienced as my senses were coming alive. It could have been the first time I saw the beautiful bay of Parga as I walked up its ancient steps to the castle, where it seemed that nature, history, and time all collided in the present, as I stood at the top of the fortified hill looking down on the bay. Or tasting the fresh bread from the bakery, feeling the cobblestones beneath my flip flops, marveling at the colors of the buildings along the waterfront. Perhaps it was in another ancient city, Tropea; feeling free as we planted ourselves at a street-side bar drinking mojitos all night, where I borrowed the band's guitar to play for the crowd. I was an observer, a wanderer, a sailor, a rock star. I was nobody – and nobody was exactly who I needed to be at that moment in my life.

HOW LONG HAD I BEEN RUNNING ON EMPTY?

September, 2018
Detroit to San Diego

Music has a unique way of speaking to us that can push past emotions, even when they are far from the surface. It reaches somewhere deeper inside of us where truth dwells and provides a sense of unadulterated experience. It seems to build a superhighway along which our emotions travel from deep inside to the surface. Have you ever heard a song that makes you cry? Have you thought about why it's possible for someone else's words to touch your soul?

For some reason, upon my return to Detroit, I found myself downloading Jackson Browne songs. I kept hitting replay over and over on two songs: *Doctor My Eyes* and *Running on Empty*. The moisture in my tears evaporated back into the atmosphere as emotions flew down that superhighway inside of my soul. Not surprisingly, both songs are reflective of life. Out of the blue, *these songs found me* and helped me process more of the past while moving into the future. All I had been doing since May was reflecting on my life. Frankly, I wasn't sure how much more self-honesty I could tolerate. If I had known that it would be another six months of self-examination, I might have given up and returned to the ego soothing deception which for years had been my sustenance.

As I listened to *Doctor My Eyes*, I reflected on the difficulty in trying to see things as they really were while I worked in a leadership role. Sometimes, it's hard to make the best of things you really don't believe in. Over time, it had become increasingly difficult to represent those decisions to others both inside and outside the company. Fighting for what you believe are just causes can be exhausting. Fighting induces weariness, and weariness is another version of surrender. Once you stop fighting, it becomes easier and easier to accept things in opposition to your values. Sometimes, it's because you benefit from it, and other times, maybe you're just tired of fighting, so you comply. You "go along to get along," as the saying goes. Reasons for my exit had become increasingly clear as time passed. If I had stayed, would I have lost the ability to feel *anything?*

It was time to point my car to the west. Along the way, I listened to the lyrics of Running on Empty as the corn fields of Iowa flew by outside my window as fast as the decades in my life. My 20s, 30s and 40s were suddenly gone. These were the same cornfields that I had seen three years earlier during the trip from California to Detroit, when I had been hopeful about so much. The memories came back to me as I drove on from past to future. Uncertainty was on the road ahead and lingered around in my rearview mirror. I didn't even really know what I was expecting to find when I got back "home."

Home had never been a real thing for me; I had moved twenty times in the first eighteen years of my life, which had included Pennsylvania, California, Canada, and Ireland. Home was usually where I was moving to, not where I was from. Maybe that's why I identified so deeply with the lyrics of the song. I had been running for my entire life, and I really didn't understand why, or even what road I had been on. I knew these were the questions I had to answer, I just didn't understand how. After being off work for three months, and despite having so much time to sail and wander, I was still running on an empty tank.

How does our tank get so empty? Companies preach work-life balance, but executives and managers email you at 10:00 p.m. because that's when it's convenient for *them*. What message does that send? We answer the email, from the couch at home, the hotel room, or the airport, because the machine is always in the palm of our hands. It's there to wake us up, to remind us of our to-do list, to entertain us, navigate for us, ostensibly to enrich our lives; a constant connection to everything. Thoreau wrote, "Our inventions...are but improved means to an unimproved end..." Are we really better off with all of our advancements? It's now considered normal to work a little bit on vacation, take a quick call at a little league game, and be on our phone and computer during an "in-person" meeting. How do we end up exhausted? *How could we not?* The answer is in the palm of our hand. Our own behaviors, the expectations of others, and technology have become an unholy trinity which demands our time and attention at its altar. We seem to willingly offer the sacrifices demanded as if we have no other clear choice.

For those of us that lean toward extremes, it's easy to see how these new 'normal' things work even harder against us. We expect ourselves to answer the email, even when the sender may not have that same expectation. The thought of disconnecting, of not having the phone on and near us is, for some people, a documented cause of anxiety. When do we take a break? How can we refill our gas tank?

Jackson's vocals roared with the screeching slide guitar coming in like an orchestra to add even more color to the sunset I watched over the Colorado Rockies. I was driving west, into the sun, toward my future, but still feeling somehow behind - like I could never really get to where I was trying to go. It was all such a massive undoing and undertaking.

My phone didn't ring all the time anymore, there were no more days of sorting through one or two hundred emails over dinner. Now, I was just playing music to heal my tired soul while the road flew by under my tires. I wasn't sure yet if I missed it, or if I was glad that it was all gone.

WHERE DO I BEGIN?

January 31, 2019
Terminal F9, Atlanta Hartsfield International Airport

Terminal F9. In all my years of traveling, this is the only terminal number I remember. The nondescript, unremarkable, international terminal, sitting next to the standard airport gift shop is the one I remember - because this is the place where I started writing this book. It seems odd that such sterile airport concrete, glass, and metal created the backdrop for such a pivotal, colorful moment in my life, but we don't often choose the time and place where these shifts occur. They seem to find us when everything has fallen apart, or when it is finally coming together. The assembly of drinking vacationers, families going home, and various business travelers were my wholly uninterested audience in the opening of this scene of the play.

A 40-liter Gill duffle bag sat at my feet with my life jacket/harness tethered to the outside, along with the three-foot cylindrical tube which carried the open ocean chart that we would use for a backup to the electronic navigation. I wore a pair of Royal Robbins travel pants, flip flops, and an old T-shirt. The bag contained a bathing suit, a few shorts and T-shirts, toiletries, and one book. That's it – that's all that I wanted for a one-month voyage on a forty-four foot sailboat.

It had been eight months since I had left my job. Eight months to wind down, wander, process and begin to rebuild. Here I was, waiting to board a plane to Panama, where I would meet a crew and sail to the French Marquesas. I was ready to cross an ocean.

An ocean passage was something I had dreamt about for most of my life, and for so many years it seemed out of reach. The passage from Panama to Polynesia is one of the more notable passages for sailors who document their journeys. For me, it would be a journey of firsts: my first long open ocean passage, seeing the Southern Cross for the first time, knowing the feeling of making landfall after a month at sea, and finally seeing myself for who I am.

For years, there were barriers to an ocean passage that existed only in my mind. We set limits upon ourselves; we accept the limits that others set. We allow fear to become our master, which ultimately becomes our prison guard. There are myriad reasons why people don't do the things they want. They allow life, fear, money, and misplaced priorities to stop them from pursuing dreams. It's easy to give in and give up.

There are the "never leavers" - people who will never leave because there is always something else to be done on the boat. Underneath that perfectionism lies the real reasons they will never admit. At some point you have to decide which is more terrifying, dying in a storm at sea, or dying at home knowing you were too afraid to leave the safe harbor.

A combination of time, training, and tenacity had finally broken down my barriers. It was my turn to follow in the footsteps of famous sailors that had gone before me like Slocum, Baldwin, Powels, and others whose stories I had read. I had dreamt of sailing a small sailboat across the South Pacific Ocean on a 4,000 nautical mile voyage. I spent my days and nights dreaming of the journeys of others, while letting my own dreams take shape. Those dreams kept me alive through long, boring meetings, seclusion, and snowy days in Michigan. My curiosity of what it was like 'out there' was close to being satisfied.

Surely, with this monumental voyage in front of me, I wondered, would I finally be able to write what I felt and observed? Hesitantly, my gaze went down to the journal in my bag. With so many false starts over the last eight months, should I even bother? Like a wind that whispered my name, the journal seemed to beg me to write something. How do you describe a juncture and a journey so profound when there is a lifetime of context that came before it? The very task of deciding how to start seemed overwhelming. The book couldn't just be about the sailing. Sailing was the backdrop. This story is about coming to terms with a lifetime of self-neglect and dishonesty with myself. These were the things I didn't want to admit, let alone write and share with others. I knew what needed to be written down. My hands forced open the journal and hesitantly, I wrote the words, "I bought myself a year."

Then, I wrote the following three questions about the journey I was taking.

1. What if nothing changes?
2. What if something changes?
3. What if everything changes?

Which of those questions inspired the most fear in me? If nothing changed, my life would be stuck in a rut. If some things changed, I'd spend my life trying to achieve balance between different worlds. If everything changed, everything would have to be examined, truths faced that had long been ignored. The last one was the scariest. Honesty would require me to take down the protective layers of ego that had been built up over so many years; to be myself at a time when I had no idea what that even meant. I continued with some notes about "self-honesty" – a term I was using to describe what was happening inside of me. For the last eight months, I had been pulling away all the dishonest constructs that were the framework which had supported my world. Most of it was gone, but threads of it were still holding me up, precariously and tenuously.

There was nothing else I wanted to write that day. Staring at the questions for a few minutes before closing the journal, it occurred to me that the words that I had written were imperfect, like me, but at least they were *mine*. They weren't littered with success psychology, corporate babble, or vain attempts to be someone else. They weren't quite completely honest – but I was getting closer. Soon I would be offshore, where the lies would be easier to see.

WHAT AM I REALLY PREPARING FOR?

February 1, 2019
Panama City, Panama

After a good night's sleep in the last air conditioning I would feel for over a month, I packed up my duffle bag, double checked all my documents, and headed to the lobby. Stepping off the elevator, I looked over to see a tall, lanky fellow with unkempt hair, wearing a T-shirt and shorts. His name was Simon, the owner of *Antares*. He had the look of an experienced sailor - someone who had been living on a boat for a while. It was equally as easy for him to spot me carrying the chart case, lifejacket, and Gill duffle bag. We both looked out of place on the highly polished marble floors, surrounded by nice restaurants and glass elevators. Our eyes met with a simple, knowing smile and nod. We shook hands quickly, I handed him some of my things, and went over to the counter to check out. The clock was ticking, and we had a lot to do in the next two days.

Simon told me that the "hire car" (British term for a rental) was outside. We put my things in the trunk and piled into the small car, where Felipe, the third member of *Antares*' crew waited. When he shook my hand, he smiled warmly; the first hint of his jovial and kind nature. Simon had been sailing *Antares* for several years by this time, and he was on the last leg of his journey. By the time he finished, he would have sailed more than halfway around the world. Part of his journey had been with his wife and kids, and part of it with strangers like me, who would help him sail his vessel. Felipe had shown up in Panama a few days before, looking to hitch a ride on a boat crossing the Pacific. At thirty something, he had figured life out so much sooner than I had. At fifty-four years old, I was still trying to determine my course; learning to separate the the basics from things that really mattered in life. Three complete strangers were about to board a small boat and cross a large ocean. Our only common bond was a love of the canvas, the sea, and adventure.

The day's itinerary was reviewed with me as we wound our way through the chaotic streets of Panama. We were to make stops at a ship's chandlery, power tool supply store, shopping mall, port customs, and complete one of three provisioning trips before we headed back to the boat. It was a bold agenda given that it was already 10:00 a.m. It was declared in such a manner as to be unimpeachable, that lunch would be at McDonald's. This event was enthusiastically anticipated by Simon because it had been some time since he had visited the Golden Arches, and it would be an exceptionally long time before he saw another one. With the vast expanse of South Pacific Ocean before us, we took all of our tasks seriously. We would have to live with our decisions regarding these matters for the next month. With each stop, the tiny car started to fill up with all that we would need for our journey.

As we navigated the busy streets, it was stunning to see such abject poverty in a country that controlled the door between the Atlantic and the Pacific Oceans; a country with so much potential and influx of capital. The gap between the rich and the poor is very wide, and it was easy to experience the impact of this chasm as we drove along Panama's highways. Shanty towns, where trash – much of it plastic – was just thrown from a second story window to create a vast plastic mountain below the building. It was shocking, disturbing, and unlike anything I had ever seen up close. I pondered the question of how much longer the world could go on with an ever-increasing gap between rich and poor. Some of what I had seen and experienced over the last year made me wish I were still living in ignorance. My life had for some time been one of the American white, upper-middle class - we had a nice home on "Easy Street." Wonderful neighborhoods, little crime, good schools, youth sports – the works. Seeing such poverty in a country that should have economic opportunity made me aware that the illusion in which I had lived was protected by only a thin veil of ignorance. I guess I couldn't admit that places like this existed in the United States: neighborhoods without sewage treatment and homes without running water in the wealthiest and most powerful nation on earth. It's easy to hide from this reality if you choose to do so - just keep ingesting the image of "Great America" which is pushed by businesses, politicians, and even some media outlets. It's easy to be so busy with life, that we have no time to see the world in which we live. It's insanity to think that we are not all interconnected and interdependent in fundamental ways.

The day wore on. Each errand was taking longer than anticipated due to the language barriers and bureaucratic systems in place at these stores. At the tool store, you selected the item from a display; then the sales person wrote out a ticket by hand that you took to a cashier, who rang up the item and took your payment. Finally, you took your receipt to another window where someone picked your item and stamped your receipt. These antiquated processes added time to each stop, and we began to see the day slipping away from us with so much yet undone.

We continued with our list of things to acquire, which now included my very important six bags of Panamanian coffee – I would leave the dock without a lot of things, but not without coffee! Along the way we drove through some beautiful older neighborhoods which stood in stark contrast to the slums we had passed through earlier. Two worlds – the haves and the have nots – were becoming an all too familiar scene I had witnessed in the last year. I had seen half-billion dollar super yachts (yes, half-billion) resting at anchor next to people who lived a hand-to-mouth existence. It has always been this way in the world, but we are living in an era where the rich aren't just getting richer, they are getting *much* richer, and the poor are falling faster behind. I feared that Panama could be a dystopian poster for the future of the United States if we didn't make some corrections to our course as a nation.

After we had dutifully cleared out of customs, we began the drive back up the coast toward the marina where *Antares* rested before her long journey. It was only about a forty-mile drive, but the traffic was as thick as a Los Angeles freeway at rush hour. We crept slowly along until we finally broke free from the city. It was dark now, so I wouldn't get my first view of the Panamanian countryside until the next day. Small towns along the way echoed the poverty of Panama City. I wondered if the existence of the quaint provincial Central American town was real, or if that was just some bullshit that Hollywood had sold me. Whatever the case, the things I had hoped to find were clearly not to be found in there. It left me wondering if I would find them on the other side of the Pacific, or if I would never find them at all.

Although it was late, we decided to make the provisioning stop anyway. Outside of the city, we stopped at a giant warehouse grocery store. Without much regard to how much room was left in the "hire car," which now contained my baggage, power tools, coffee, and Felipe's new ukulele, we grabbed two carts and started filling them like squirrels gathering nuts for the winter. The trip was becoming more of a reality in my mind as we ran quick computations about the number of days at sea, how many jars of this or cans of that we would need and the importance of each decision. Compromises were made and agreements reached on everything from cereal to Spam. There were no convenience stores along the way on this journey. We expected the trip to last at least three weeks, but probably four. It would be the longest passage any of us had ever made. While I had read dozens of books about that crossing, and it had been done by countless others before me, somehow I still felt like I was heading out into the unknown.

The feeling that I was preparing for two journeys started sinking in. This wasn't only a journey across an ocean, but a journey into who I was, and who I would become. After years of self-denial and corporate nonsense that had in many ways defined me, I wanted to find out who "I" really was. The prospect of that inward journey scared me a hell of a lot more than crossing the ocean. I wondered if Simon and Felipe would have been so quick to accept me if my sailing resume had also said, "Thirty-five years of sailing experience and a captain's license, polluted by fifty-four years of a poorly managed life, with a fair amount of emotional damage." It certainly would have been fair for them to pass on the opportunity to sail with such a rare gem. However, looking back now, and knowing the character of those men, I think the answer would have been in the affirmative from both. Simon might have said, "Let's go mate! We'll sort it out on the crossing." And Felipe, in his ever-accepting manner would have simply said in his Portuguese accented English, *"Eeets normal my friend."* They too were on journeys and understood that our imperfections were as vast as the ocean we would cross, and that by working together, we were far better off than being alone.

TRUTH OR DARE?

February 4, 2019
Aboard *Antares*
06° 03 north
80° 24 west
Approximately 200 miles Southeast of Vista Mar Marina, Panama

Do you remember the game of "Truth or Dare" that we played as kids? When it was your turn you would be given the choice of answering a question truthfully or doing a dare. For me, this journey was both a truth and a dare. We had left Panama without any fanfare, no crowds waving goodbye, and we played no anthems on the stereo. Three simple men set out to cross a large ocean. Truth awaited me in the ocean which had dared me to cross it.

We were well on our way toward the Galapagos Islands which was the first waypoint in our journey. While *Antares* wasn't planning a stop there, it was comforting to know that just a few hundred miles away, civilization lay with its comforts and protections. Once past the Galapagos we would be on our own until we reached the Marquesas.

When we think of an emergency in our daily lives, we know that first responders can be at our door in minutes. The term *emergency* takes on a different meaning at sea. In the middle of the ocean, there is no 911, and even if someone picks up your distress signal, it may be days or weeks before you receive help, if ever. At one point we found an old life ring floating in the water bearing the illegible name of a ship. What had happened to her? Had someone fallen in, and was this ring tossed to them? We would never know; we could only wonder.

By our second night out of Panama I had settled into the routine of the boat and the sea. There is a cadence in the natural order, and I found it best to flow with it rather than fight against it.

I rose along with the sun. It was a time of newness and light, and a chance to see the beautiful desolation that surrounded us each day. In that first moment when you entered the world above deck, you would see what things darkness had hidden from your view during the long night watch. Most mornings on this part of the journey through the Intertropical Convergence Zone, I would come on deck to view a sea of glass all the way to the horizon. Some mornings, there were widely spaced rolling hills of water that looked like a view of plains without the grass. Somewhere in the sky, clouds completed the canvas spread out before me.

There are tasks to be completed, food must be prepared, and *Antares* must be cleaned. Simple, daily life. Making coffee, and then sipping it while taking in all of this beauty, with no pressure to "get going" or be somewhere else. I was learning to just be *here* wherever *here* happened to be at that moment: washing dishes, tidying up the crew area - nothing too heavy.

The afternoons brought a chance to rest and enjoy the crew and ocean while we all pursued individual pastimes: Felipe played his ukulele, Simon listened to his 'tunes' and read a bit, and I observed everything intensely, contemplating all of it: the ocean, the sea birds, the sky, the boat, the crew, the rhythm, and my place in all of it. The vastness of the expanse was simultaneously awe inspiring and terrifying.

Eventually, the sun began its descent over the horizon. Order and routine occupied a special place on our long journey. Simon would call for a daily imbibement of rum and coke, which became a ritual and a game under his watchful humor. "Felipe, it's time for rhuuuuummm." The call would come for the beverage as the sun began to set. In his always giving and generous manner, Felipe would prepare the beverages. We sat together as a crew, a family, and watched the day transform to night with splendor unknown.

During the hours the sun was down, we each performed a night watch. Watches were broken down into 9:00 p.m. - 12:00 a.m., 12:00 a.m. - 3:00 a.m., and 3:00 a.m. - 6:00 a.m. I often chose the 12:00 a.m. – 3:00 a.m. watch, because it allowed me to take a short nap first, and it provided me with solitude unparalleled to anything I had ever known.

One night, I sat on deck in that solitude as a soft wind blew gently on my bare chest, and opened my journal to write. I wanted to record that moment, to somehow capture on paper what all of my senses felt, and the wellspring of emotion coming to life inside of me. But I knew that in order to get to the present, I must face the past. Despite my desire to ignore or bury it, I had to employ a mental shovel and dig. It was time to wholly consider the things that had led me to this point in my life, both good and bad. Self-examination was the only way for me to ensure I would not repeat past mistakes or, in willful ignorance, find myself suffering the ill-effects of the diseases that could hide inside my mind and heart.

What had I said about myself to others? What had I said to myself? I would be the prosecutor and the jury in this inquiry. The witness list would include the many faces I had worn, and the consequences they had on my life and others. Some would be found guilty, and then sentenced. Others were pardoned. Very few were acquitted.

When we can't seem to bear the truth, we concoct stories to support our view of the world around us, instead of simply acknowledging the truth and changing our point of view. A lifetime of doing this can leave you somewhat distant from reality. I'm sure it's embedded in our DNA as humans evolved and attempted to explain the world we lived in - to somehow make sense of it, to ensure we survive. For me, reality was as far away as the islands we sailed towards. To find my life, to find the islands, direction and accurate navigation would be critical.

Lies and arrogance began to collapse under the weight of the passage. There is no room for falsehoods on the ocean, for it demands respect, and respect means truthfulness. Truth and fiction in my life had to be separated, by force if necessary; I had become unwilling to allow fiction in any part of my life. No more self-soothing stories were to be told. The dare of crossing the ocean would be every day for the next thirty-two days; it had become the dare of facing the truth. Truth or Dare had become Truth *and* Dare. Surrounded by water, there would be no escape from this game.

NOTHING ELSE MATTERS

February 8, 2019
Aboard *Antares*
0° 05 north
86°48 west
Approximately 200 Nautical Miles Northeast of the Galapagos.

It was 2:45 a.m. when my iPhone alarm jolted me from an existence in another world, where the soft sounds of *Antares* slipping through the calm sea found their way into my dreams. After pulling on a T-shirt that was getting ripe, I gathered up my things, and made my way on-deck for the 3:00 a.m. to 6:00 a.m. watch. As my head slid through the hatch, I was greeted by Felipe's warm smile and trademark, "Hey, Broooo." Still waking up, I smiled and nodded, then said, "Man it's dark tonight." He motioned with his arm to the sky and said, "Eeets a new moon," in his thick accent. To Felipe the moon is a magical woman to be gazed upon, pondered, and revered; a love so genuine it could turn even the most ardent city dweller into a naturalist.

In my life of rushing to success, I had managed to completely miss all the details about the moon; one of the many things I missed. I had a lot of things to make up for in whatever time I had left. While Felipe was schooling me on her beauty, he was teaching me even more about life. The lesson at hand was *slow it down... enjoy this moment... it won't last forever.* I watched as he completed his evening ritual of carefully packing up all his belongings into a well-worn backpack that told the story of his journeys and adventures in life. When finished, he offered a gentle, "'Night, Brooo," and disappeared into the dark cavern of the *Antares* saloon.

I began thinking about the long journey ahead of us, about thirty-two hundred miles left to travel at this point. I projected my thoughts forward to that last day of the trip when someone would call, "Land, Ho!" When would we see Hiva Oa appear over the horizon? With this picture in my mind, the questions began: What will it be like? How will I feel? Will I be happy or sad that the trip is over? Questions such as these had occupied my mind since I decided, *someday I will go.* This catechization continued until I was satisfied with the answers and my mind thoroughly exhausted.

Hiva Oa is a small island in the French Marquesas, a remote island group that lies on the eastern edge of Polynesia. Few people outside of the sailing community have heard of it, because it's so small. Sailors are well-acquainted with the Marquesas because it's the first land west of the Galapagos Islands - about three thousand miles west. I felt as if a magnetic force was pulling me toward the islands, as if it was a required stop on my journey through life. I didn't understand why.

At this point in our passage, we were well into the Doldrums, the area defined as five degrees of latitude north and south of the equator. It's an area that sailors dread because we are nothing more than drifting objects without the wind. In this narrow band around the equator, the winds are light and unpredictable – two traits that riders of the wind find frustrating beyond description. Doldrums is an Old English word used to describe a mood that was both lethargic and gloomy. That's the way sailors feel when they have no wind, it has a nearly immediate effect on the mind and soul. Over time, sailors began to use the term to define this region near the equator, because its winds gave them the doldrums. This place, where a sailing ship with no wind could be left drifting for days or weeks, also happens to inconveniently be located in an area of stifling heat because of its proximity to the equator. This is where sailors could become mutinous, insane, or filled with hatred and fear; it possesses the ability to bring out the worst in humanity, but also the best. For this place is where sailors also might find the courage to beat back inner demons pushing them to the brink.

Admittedly, one of the reasons I made the trip was an attempt to purify my weary soul. It was a religious pilgrimage of sorts, the kind that could work on a sailor's heart. My life until last summer had become so comfortable, polished, easily controlled, and painfully predictable. I had grown unaccustomed to physical hardships and missed the value that they brought to my mind. There was no longer any triumph through endurance that I had found in my youth – unless of course we were to count my endurance through endless, pointless meetings or a never-ending inbox of emails. Those experiences created the buildup of disgust and contempt that had taken over my life, and this ocean was the place for it to be cleansed.

After four days in the grasp of the Doldrums, the definition was becoming all too real. We ran the engine a few times when we had no wind at all, but we all agreed it was better to hold our fuel in reserve for an emergency. We became increasingly grateful for the favorable current which added to our speed in the very light wind; it made our tedious progress through the region almost bearable. We couldn't measure the exact speed of the current because the paddle wheel that measured speed was broken. There were a lot of things on *Antares* which were broken. I was one of them.

Our concern of using fuel to speed the journey was soon replaced by my concern of running out of water due to an indefinite increase in our time at sea. There was no water-maker aboard – what we had is what we brought. Every decision to use water, both personally, and as a group, was carefully considered. Dishes were washed with saltwater and rinsed with a small basin of fresh water pulled out with the cupped palms of our hands. Small splashes of fresh water were all we could spare. Showers and laundry were done with saltwater also. If there was a little hot water left in the kettle, it would be used again; not a drop was wasted. We found ourselves frequently glancing over at the circuit breaker to make sure that the water pump remained switched off when not in use, so that a leaky faucet wouldn't put our lives in danger. The fact that our world was now dominated by the water on which we journeyed seem to inflame the irony of its abundant uselessness to sustain our lives.

By 4:30 a.m., the wind had increased slightly, and was blowing gently on my right shoulder blade as I leaned back against the port side of the cockpit, telling me without looking at the instruments that we were on a broad reach, meaning that the wind was slightly behind us and coming over our port quarter. My eyes without thought glanced up at the sails to see if they were at an optimal angle for that point of sail. It had taken many years, but there had been a definite shift in my approach to sailing that had gone from thinking, to doing, to being. When we learn, we are using our minds. Thinking: there are terms to remember, patterns to follow, and a system of process honed by centuries of experience that came before us. Then, after learning, we apply our knowledge. Doing: our minds instruct our bodies in an ever-increasing degree of speed and accuracy. After we have learned and done, there is an effortless state where we realize our belonging to all of it. Being: the point at which we are part of the wind, the sail, the helm, and we sense our connection to all of it. Thinking no longer requires effort, doing no longer requires thinking, and being just *is* – it had become as natural as breathing. I was working in harmony with the environment and the boat, not fighting against them.

My mind shifted from the endless questions I had been considering over the last hour and a half, and I began to let my senses take over for the rest of the watch. The journal lay open before me as I jotted down some of the moments and considered my life up to that point. Having been given just one life, I was glad that I had taken this journey. Despite that gladness, there was a sense of simultaneous apprehension and relief occurring inside of me. I still did not know where all of this would lead me – I still had not set my course.

Sitting and listening to the water running gently beneath *Antares*, I gazed down at the dark water disturbed by our wake and watched as it splashed and lit up with bioluminescent life. I continued to watch this for some time, with the fascination of a child seeing a magic trick; the planet opens the curtain for another breathtaking performance. It's quite possible that this natural beauty could have occupied the remaining time on my watch, had it not been interrupted by a new character entering onto this ocean-theatre's stage.

Without warning, I heard a loudly distinct waterspout somewhere behind the boat, to my estimate, about fifty feet. But since it was pitch black, it was impossible to see anything that was more than a few feet away. Straining my eyes as if they could somehow pierce the darkness,

I looked for what I thought was a dolphin. I called to him, "Hey there, come over and say hello!" No matter how hard I tried, I couldn't see anything. Then, moments later, I saw a bioluminescent, dolphin-sized green blob rushing underwater toward *Antares*. The second before it would have slammed into the side of the boat, it dove underneath and disappeared. After a few minutes, I heard his spout and he came back for his encore performance, as I laughed with delight.

In a life that had consisted of commutes, cubicles, airplanes, emails, teleconferences, meetings, endless PowerPoints, and weekend exhaustion while "catching up," nothing compared to this moment. Never before, had nature made such an impact on my soul. As I sat there in amazement, I wondered why I had worked so hard to be a success, to the detriment and degradation of all other aspects of life. How had that singular focus resulted in my forfeiture of this kind of experience? *Was it worth it?* This moment in my life seemed infinitely more successful than any professional achievement, and certainly worth more in terms of inherent value than anything I had amassed in my 401k. My priorities were being reshaped by the forces of nature. It was as if everything had come into focus as the universe spoke to me three words - *nothing else matters.*

CONTROL IS AN ILLUSION

Aboard *Antares*
West of the Galapagos Islands

As the days passed, marked only by the sun's rising and setting, realizations about life - my life - were coming to the forefront of my mind. My ideas had been too small and all the limits I thought were real were only self-imposed. Most importantly, I came to realize that the idea that we have any real control in this life is an absolute illusion.

Being in the middle of an ocean has a way of reframing your point of view on many of life's matters; control is no exception. Throughout my life, I had periodically reminded myself that we live on a planet that is spinning at close to one-thousand miles per hour on a comparatively thin crust of dirt, above a core of molten metal almost as hot as the sun. This little fact has a way of putting my concerns in perspective and increases my trust in the natural order. If I am going to worry about my life, being terrified of spinning through space on a hot ball of metal would be a good place to start. If I am not going to worry about that – why should I worry about anything? All my problems and concerns begin to pale in comparison. Once I freed my mind from worry and an attempt to control everything, my load lightened, and I was finally able to see the moments around me with greater clarity.

On *Antares*, the fact that control is an illusion is lived out each moment of each day. At any moment a rogue wave could appear from nowhere and wipe us from the face of the earth. We could hit a shipping container and sink, lose the wind, or run out of water and die of thirst. The list goes on and on. For those on a sailboat making passage, one could easily occupy every second of the day worrying about something. The ocean was my schoolmaster and its lesson was clear: *You are not in control; you can only influence outcomes.*

The need to control is a shifty and often elusive foe to battle. No doubt it is based in our evolution, Maslow's hierarchy of needs, and framed by our past. I believe that my own need for perfection and control is rooted in my growing up in a home with alcoholism and mental illness. My childhood memories are punctuated by traumatic events: Mom attempting suicide twice, Dad being in the locked unit of a psychiatric ward, Mom setting Dad's motorcycle on fire in the driveway, a guy from Vegas showing up at our home and looking for my dad to settle his gambling debt, my brother losing his leg, and my father's sudden death. All of that happened before I turned fifteen. We moved twenty times in eighteen years. I attended four different elementary schools, two middle schools, and two high schools. I guess I wanted to control things in my life because everything in my childhood world had been so very out of control. I learned to wait in desperate anticipation for the other shoe to drop, as if somehow my apprehension would prepare me for the reality of what would happen next. Fear and ego reappear in the realm of control, and you can't control one without controlling the other. The underlying fear that something might happen is a reason to attempt to control things in our world.

As parents of young children, my wife and I were desperate to keep our kids safe, so we would pile them into the car and drive them to school. It never occurred to us that this choice simply changes the possibility of *what may happen*, but not *if something will happen*. Safely buckled into the car, we are safe from one type of harm, not all types of harm. We are never safe from all types of harm. Our ego benefits when we maintain the illusion of control because we are reassured of our place and station in life. My marriage is hunky-dory, my kid is on the honor roll, and I'm a star at work. Pride. Ego. Then, you may see a text on your spouse's phone from the other significant other, the principal calls you and tells you that your kid was caught smoking pot at school, and you get downsized at work. Humility. Ego damage. Any of this can happen, all of the time. Settle in for the ride.

There are many people with the dream of sailing across an ocean. Some go as far as buying a boat. Most never leave the harbor. Some never leave the dock. After taking a costly and important step to follow a dream, excuses will start to pop up all around them. "Well, we've got this really big project at work right now, we should wait until it's over." "Our son just had a baby; we don't want to be so far away." "The boat isn't ready; we need to install a new ____." After the new ____ is installed, then there will be another ____ that will need to be replaced. Next, they are running over budget and need to stop, or maybe a spouse gets sick; the list goes on. Control, fear, and ego will get in the way. Life will get in the way unless you do everything you can to stop it, unless you take every chance you get to live it. Dum vivimus vivamus is a Latin phrase that translates to *while we are living, let us live*.

Simon, the owner of *Antares*, shared his perspective with us while we crossed the ocean. In his estimation, it's better to leave mostly ready than to wait until everything is perfect because you may never leave the dock. If something happens, part of the experience is "sorting it out" as he would say in his British accent. I asked him once why he chose to make this trip, "We are a long-time dead" was all that he said in reply. It's all that was needed to be said, so profound were those words, they will mark my life until I too will be "a long-time dead." Simon left England much in the same way countless others had done before him. We left Panama just after and right before dozens of others.

None of it is perfect. Perfection is an illusion that wastes our time, money, and energy. Some people travel on multi-million dollar boats with a hundred thousand dollars' worth of electronics, safety gear, satellite communications, and a myriad of other things to keep them 'safe.' Other people leave on a fifty-year old boat they bought for five thousand bucks on Craigslist, with a handheld VHF radio, Garmin GPS, and a twenty-year-old chart. The same rogue wave could sink either of those boats.

I guess we must answer these questions: what do I fear the most, dying, or not ever living? What is worse, dying quickly doing something you love, or dying slowly wishing you had taken more chances? In my final estimation, life is to be lived. Control, fear, and ego will interfere - only if I allow them to.

My past, present and future seemed to collide in the middle of the ocean. I was never in control. When I thought I was, it was merely an illusion. Tomorrow may or may not come. I took some chances and placed a few big bets, and now my life is forever my own.

Felipe explains his view of life like this, "Just walk my friend, and the universe will take care of everything else." So, walk I will.

WHAT DOES IT MEAN FOR SOMETHING TO BE PERFECT?

February 14, 2019
Aboard *Antares*
4° south
97° 48 west

After twelve days at sea, the reality of being on the open ocean was setting in. It's hard to imagine the experience of being completely isolated from the rest of the world by such a vast barrier. During the years that I had spent dreaming about this long passage, I had tried to imagine what it would feel like being out on the ocean, so far from civilization. Reality was dramatically different than anything I'd imagined. It isn't just the realization that you are isolated, it is the continued state of isolation as each day slowly passes while you travel at five or six nautical miles per hour.

Imagine yourself crossing the United States on a bicycle at a very leisurely pace. Now picture yourself about one-third of the way, realizing that you still have another twenty days ahead of you. Finally, you look around you, and instead of roads, towns, and people, you see nothing but cornfields and clouds. That is all you will see for the next twenty days.

Simon, as the owner of *Antares*, set the tone for the trip. Always relaxed and casual, he seemed unwilling to take anything too seriously unless it *really* mattered. He had a good measure of what mattered and what didn't. He periodically entertained us with an impression, or a humorous story, sometimes just appearing on deck as a different character, such as a waiter at a Chinese restaurant. I found his whimsical approach to life alluring and realized he was yet another role model set before me.

Everything doesn't have to be perfect before you can take a break and enjoy the moment. *Antares*, my shipmates (with their devil-may-care attitudes), and the journey itself were teaching me this perspective. The lesson was simple, *Cam, it's okay to relax*. There were many things on the boat that needed attention (at least in my mind). I could see disorganization in a cupboard, in our provisions, in the main saloon, and in stowage areas. I struggled to understand how Simon and Felipe could walk by them without the slightest bit of concern, then go out on deck and enjoy the day. I realized that they understood something which had eluded me for most of my life – everything doesn't have to be perfect before you can relax.

I had spent a ridiculous amount of my life trying to perfect things around me. I can't even remember most of them, which at the time, were so important that they were prioritized over sleep, food, and people. I certainly appreciate order, cleanliness, and a minimalistic approach, but even good things can be taken too far. It seems unsurprising in retrospect that a childhood of chaos compelled me to create order. It's another means of establishing the illusion of control. There was a drive inside of me to perfect whatever task I was working on to the exclusion of all other things. All would be subjugated to the completion of the task. Once it was done, I could relax. Until of course, I noticed something else that needed my attention. The time spent re-shuffling a closet of stuff is gone and can never be regained. I'm not saying you shouldn't clean your closet once in a while. Cleaning a closet should fit in the context of a life well-lived; it should not be *the thing* which governs your life.

I wasted time which could have been better spent simply enjoying life. I was learning each day on this passage that everything is not perfect, nor does it have to be. I could enjoy the day even if there was chaos around me – and you can't get more chaotic than the middle of the ocean. Random. Chaos. Beauty. Peace. These are words that don't seem to belong next to each other but actually do, for they are an apt description of our world.

We had spent the last two days in a storm which had been a welcome event, because it moved us faster toward our destination. We were able to make our course almost due south and we were finally heading out of the Doldrums. It wouldn't be much longer before we made our turn to the west, and with that turn would be our long-awaited marriage to the trade winds.

The storm had been an ally to progress and an enemy of comfort. Sleeping meant feeling the force of *Antares* as she slammed into waves, or moments of weightlessness as we dropped down off a crest of a never-ending group of waves. Somehow water was getting into the forward cabins. Water inside the boat is always concerning until you know where it's coming from - I stood in a puddle wondering, "What the hell?" The berth cushions, bedding, and most of our clothes were soaked. Random. Chaos.

When the rain finally passed, we glided along quickly on a fresh breeze and alongside ten-foot swells, the last remnant of the storm. As the sun came up, the ocean revealed its deep blue hue as the wind brushed off the white tops of the swells and caused them to burst into a thousand beautiful sparkles in the sunshine. The sun worked to warm the boat, and we used the opportunity to put the wet cushions and our clothes out to dry.

I had reminded myself a hundred times over the last eight months: when I am cold, eventually I will be warm; when I am hot, eventually I will be cool; when I am wet, eventually I will be dry. The feelings of discomfort were temporary, and part of the price to be paid for the adventure. The experience itself is by nature, imperfect. *Beauty. Peace.*

As the soggy gear surrounded me on deck, my ideas of perfection were once again challenged. The bunk was wet, and it smelled. There were areas of the boat that needed attention. I was surrounded by disorganization. As I took it all in, I felt the need to take *ownership* (read: take control) of the situation and *fix* everything (read: control everything). Simon seemed unfazed by any of it, and I wondered how that was even possible.

I began to wonder if Simon was some kind of Zen sailing master, concerned only with each moment. By paying attention to him, I was starting to catch on. My compulsion to put order into all that is around me was part of the illusion that had supported my life. Fear. Ego. Control. It was becoming easier for me to accept what I could not control. This was a timely realization. Because, in the middle of the ocean, the sum of what is beyond our control is immeasurable.

Since I did not yield to my demons demanding that I organize everything, I made my way on deck to hang out with Simon and Felipe.

It felt awkward at first, the act of just sitting while so much needed to be done. But I did exactly what I saw them do - sit down and relax. What I observed amazed me.

I could see the sun on the water bursting into sparkling drops, flying fish soaring out of the water for hundreds of feet, sea birds floating around us overhead, Felipe's warm smile, and Simon's impish grin. I saw all that I would have missed if I had stayed down below creating temporary order. When people say, "You can't get that moment back," it's literal. There was no way I could have recreated the first few moments of being on deck. Even if we had turned around, we couldn't have been in that exact spot, at that exact time, when that school of fish flew out of the water, and those bursts of water hit the sun at that exact angle. *To see that moment, I had to be in that moment.* There is simply no way around that truth. If I had stayed below and cleaned up, this chapter might have been titled, *Organizing a Cabinet*, which as you can only imagine, would be enthralling. The perfection I could finally see around me in real time was far better than anything that I could have created.

I was beginning to realize that everything doesn't need to meet my imaginary standard of perfection in order to function. There are times when it's okay for something to be good enough, serviceable, or tolerable. There are times when a good cleaning and organizing are needed, but I'm no longer willing to miss life in the service of another organized drawer.

While these revelations worked through my mind and soul, *Antares* sliced through the swells on her beam. She gracefully rode up the side of a ten-foot swell, crested it at a slight angle, then playfully slid down into the trough of the next swell. The dance continued thousands of times without our help. We were merely observers of nature and the laws of physics. *Antares* did what she was designed to do. She was the perfect companion for the dance. We did what we were designed to do – live.

As if on cue from a producer, a huge pod of dolphins appeared and began to herd bait fish for their evening feeding. The bait fish instinctively tried to escape while the dolphins encircled them and kept the school of fish close to each other.

While we were watching the show, we heard the high-pitched whizzing sound of our own fishing reel spooling out line as Felipe yelled, "Feeesh on" and jumped up to grab the reel. The skilled fisherman worked tirelessly to reel in the big fish. When the fight was finally over, he reached down with the gaff, pierced the tuna, and pulled it onboard – like a man right out of a Hemingway novel. Within an hour we were eating tuna curry over rice. We were all thankful for this gift from the ocean and agreed that we should not take another fish until this one was completely gone. The remnants were thrown back into the sea from which it had come, and nothing was wasted.

These were the moments I had long dreamed of and impatiently waited for: sailing across an ocean, seeing the natural world unfold before me, developing camaraderie with my mates. The whole experience could have been easily missed while toiling to make all the things around me "perfect." Perfection already surrounds us if we choose to see it.

FINALLY, I AM ALIVE

February 17, 2019
Aboard *Antares*
5° 48 south
104° 48 west
Approximately 1,500 miles due west of Ecuador

Three days later, we were on day fifteen and we still weren't halfway. We were falling behind our estimated arrival date and the psychological toll was beginning to mount. Despite the progress that we had made during and after the storm, we were slowing down again. The winds were much lighter than anticipated and progress was painfully slow. We began our passage early in the season before the trade winds normally arrive in the South Pacific. With global climates changing, it was anyone's guess as to what would happen next. We bobbed along the massive ocean and wondered if the wind would ever arrive. Our very lives depended on climate patterns as old as recorded nautical history; we remained hopeful that ours wouldn't be the story about the sailors lost at sea the year the trade winds failed to blow.

My day had started at midnight with the 12:00-3:00 a.m. watch. As on the other eleven nights, I climbed out into the cockpit, received my warm, "Hey, Bro," welcome from Felipe, got the information about the heading, the weather, the sail trim, and then watched as he completed his evening ritual of packing up. The sky was overcast, which was a sharp contrast to the clear star-filled skies and moonlit nights we had seen over the last few days. After fifteen days, fully removed from the distractions of modern life, I was becoming more in touch with the sea and the sky. Sensing the changes in the environment since the previous night, I could see and feel that the weather was changing and a storm was approaching. I assumed my favorite spot on the boat when expecting a storm, on the leeward (downwind) bench seat, with my head tucked up under the dodger, a small canvas awning that extends over a small part of the cockpit.

When the skies had been clear and starry, it was possible to rely almost completely on my visual senses. Now that the skies were dark and my vision was limited, I began exploring my other senses. I closed my eyes, listened, and felt. First, I heard the sounds of the water on the hull of *Antares* as she slid through the water. The leeward side made a *ssssshhhhh* sound which was long and smooth, while the windward (upwind) side sounded an intermittent *ch ch ch slap* sound that was choppy. In thirty-five years of sailing, this was my first time noticing the sounds on the hull and how they were different on each side. I could hear sounds in the rigging and sails telling me that the wind speed was increasing, and I could feel the wind on my bare chest. The wind which had begun as consistent and smooth, was followed by an increasingly intense slapping on my skin. All of my senses were telling me the same thing: a storm was approaching and we needed to reef the sails. I opened my eyes and went below to wake up Simon since he was next on watch and Felipe had only been asleep for about an hour, "Hey mate, sorry to wake ya, it's time to reef."

Reefing is a process of taking in a sail, so there is a reduced area of canvas exposed as the winds increase. The technique is best applied when the need is anticipated, so that the sail is already reduced by the time the stronger winds arrive. Sailors follow this rule: *the time to reef is the first time you think about it.*

We came back up on deck with our gear. When we had to leave the cockpit at night, we put on our Personal Flotation Devices (PFD) which have built-in harnesses and lifelines, which then clip onto the boat. This would help prevent us from falling overboard, or if we did, at least we would have our life jackets on. My PFD also had a clip-on water-activated light, and Personal Location Beacon that will transmit my location through global positioning satellites. Falling overboard at night in a storm ranks among the worst things that can happen to a sailor. Even with the boat moving at seven or eight knots, a crew member overboard can disappear quickly behind swells – especially on such a dark night - making it difficult, if not impossible to locate them when you turn the boat around. Our precautions were sensible, and we knew that nighttime in the ocean was no place to be careless.

The rig on *Antares* preferred a balanced approach to reefing where the headsail is reefed to the first mark, and then, if needed, the mainsail to the first reef-point, and so on for the second reef. The headsail operates on a roller furling drum, so when you are reefing the headsail, you are rolling it part of the way in. The mainsail has sewn-in points that allow you to partially lower the sail and create tension along the bottom of the sail using the reef points. The result is that you have less sail area exposed in stronger winds.

Simon began, "All right, let's reef the headsail to the first reef point and wait on the main...we'll see if the wind comes up." We had been fooled more than once. Everything would indicate that the wind was going to blow, then it would just fizzle out. "Sounds good," I replied. In sharp contrast to my days on *New Horizons*, I no longer felt the need to be right about everything, or to be in control. Simon ducked down below for a few more hours of sleep before his watch, and I returned to the exploration of my senses.

I listened again to the sound of the water on the hull, the wind in the sails and the rigging, and felt the wind on my skin. What were the sounds telling me? Was *Antares* happy with the reduced sail or should we have reefed further? Is the wind building? Periodically I would break from my exploration to record these thoughts in my journal.

For many years, I spent more time maintaining my lifestyle rather than maintaining my life: dragging myself out of bed, sitting in traffic, sitting in meetings, answering endless emails, and building another PowerPoint with all of the right buzzwords for the Senior Executives. All of this was done so that I could cash a big paycheck and pay off things I never should have purchased in the first place. I was alive only in the sense that I was still breathing and my heart was still beating.

What does it mean to be alive? That answer is different for everyone, but for me, the predictable life of a corporate calendar was dull; it was a slow march to death. Looking back, I can see that it wasn't only the corporate hustle that was killing me, it was all the faking required to succeed; smiling and nodding to ensure others knew I was "engaged," pretending to care, and tolerating nonsense. Faking it for so long left me with no idea of who I really was. I was going through the motions of what was expected of me by society, my company, my family, and some of my friends. I was trying, albeit quite poorly, to be a reflection of what I thought others wanted, and what I really needed to do was just be me – complete imperfection unhidden. I wrote the following while anchored off the Greek mainland aboard *New Horizons*: *I will never again strive to be something or someone I am not. To do so is the pinnacle of foolishness, finding yourself forever misaligned with the internal compass, seeking to please the unappeasable, and drinking continuously from an empty cup; it is to be alive without living.* I was beginning to stir back to life when I jotted down those words.

On *Antares*, playing a role is not possible because there is nowhere to hide on a forty-four-foot sailboat in the middle of the South Pacific Ocean. If I am full of shit, Simon or Felipe will spot it; they will call me out on it. If I am upset, they will ask me if I am okay and not demand that I appear to be happy. They behave this way toward me because we are a crew - our lives depend on each other. More than that, they care about me because that's just who they are. Out here, everything is real. I recall my first lesson: *the ocean is not impressed with me.* My senses are awake, my emotions honest, and not coincidentally, my anger is gone.

The watch flew by so quickly as I recorded those thoughts in my journal, that before I knew it Simon was back up for his 3:00 a.m. watch. We reefed the main and then I headed below for a few hours of choppy sleep as the bow of the boat slammed into the building seas. We had closed all the hatches in preparation for the squall, and by 6:00 a.m. it is too hot for me to stay below. I wasn't getting any sleep, so rather than trying to fight it, I embraced the morning and came back out on deck. Soon after, the three of us were drinking hot Panamanian coffee, from rich volcanic soil, and brewed in a French press. We sat contented, sipping our coffee, while we joked about the myriad of chores that we would never do. We emphasized the point that we would be relaxing on day fifteen – no different than the other fourteen, or the rest to come.

I sat shirtless watching the sky lighten at dawn. I smiled to myself as I realized *finally, I am truly alive.*

SLOWING DOWN

February 19, 2019
Aboard *Antares*
6° 00 south
109° 18 west
Approximately 1,700 miles due west of Ecuador

Puffy white cotton balls dotted a canvas of clear blue skies, perhaps the clearest I had ever seen. Something about the perspective of the open ocean, its relative flat surface, and the lack of contour from hills and buildings made the clouds appear as if they are right above the water. It looked like you could almost reach up and touch them. The winds started to back to the southeast, and confirmed that we had picked up the long-awaited trade winds. That simple change in the direction of the wind provided us with certainty and confidence. We had made the right navigational decisions, and we should start to move at a more predictable rate than we had in the Doldrums.

As I looked at those skies without anything else pulling at me, I wondered if the distractions of 24/7 entertainment have changed us as beings. Life goes rushing by in selfies and captions. Just a century ago, with no TV, internet, or computer, we might have spent an evening under the stars, perhaps alone just staring at the sky and dreaming, or conversing with a friend. Even in the middle of the ocean, there is the chance to be electronically distracted. People can bring computers and tablets filled with music, books, games, and movies. I sought a minimalistic experience with the desire to spend my days and nights observing nature, writing in my journal, and reading books. I wanted to experience an ocean passage as it was a hundred years ago. There are moments in our lives that we can never duplicate. I would never again be in that exact place, in those same circumstances. With all of our electronics, entertainment, and distractions, will we lose the ability to simply sit and reflect? Are we afraid of what we might discover about ourselves and our world once all the distractions are removed? Perhaps we need to push past what we think is boredom that causes us to reach for entertainment, and learn to explore the world around us, and within us.

On that morning I awoke with the determination to shower, which on *Antares*, required some planning. The shower was in the anchor locker on the bow of the boat. It was an act which required more than slipping into the bathroom, turning on a faucet, and hopping in. I began by gathering my towel, soap, shampoo, and clean clothes. Then squatting uncomfortably in the bathroom and reaching into the engine compartment, I opened a valve that moved saltwater to the the shower. After that, on the other side of the boat, I flipped the "on" switch that controls the pump for the shower. Finally, I made my way forward to the bow. Once I was on the bow, I opened the anchor locker that contained the shower hose. The hinge on the locker was broken, so it had to be carefully lifted up and secured it to the bow pulpit (railing) with a bungee cord. Finally, after all of that, I stripped down and hosed myself off with cold saltwater, soaped up, and rinsed off. Then, I balanced myself against the rigging and toweled off before getting dressed. Some days, I would just sit naked for a while and enjoy the cool breeze. It's a beautiful view from the bow of a boat in the middle of an ocean. Sitting there, I felt fresh and clean. Not just from the shower, but from the experience itself. My soul felt clean and my spirit refreshed. Perhaps some of the weight I had carried in life was the burden of my self-dishonesty. Since I was shedding those chains, it helped me to feel clean and free. I sat and stared off into the horizon under a clear blue sky. More time to consider life.

My meditation was delightfully interrupted as a huge pod of dolphins appeared to play in the wake of the bow of the boat. I yelled, "Dolphins in the bow wake!" Simon and Felipe popped out from behind the dodger, phones in hand, ready to get some pictures and video. I had left my phone down below, and as usual, I would enjoy the memory of this show without the ability to later post it on Facebook.

I had noticed in my travels over the last two years, that there is a difference between enjoying the moment and filming the moment. Without the camera in hand, you can experience the moment. When filming, concentration shifts to getting the best shot and on a boat, not dropping the phone in the water. As these amazing pocket computers allow us to *capture moments in time,* are we actually missing them because we are not *in the moment?*

After the shower and dolphin show, I headed back down below to do laundry. I started the process of gathering everything that would be needed: bleach, detergent, and a washbasin. I had found that hand-washing my clothes on boats brought a simplicity to my life, as it seemed to bring me into the present. Feeling the water on my hands, smelling the detergent, the tactile experience of scrubbing and wringing out each article. Ultimately bringing an appreciation for something I routinely took for granted – a clean T-shirt. I headed back out on deck to pin my clothes to the lifelines so they could dry in the sun and wind. With each chore, in each moment, I was thinking. It felt so good to just *think* without a thousand other distractions.

My reward for getting my chores done was my morning coffee, which I had uncharacteristically postponed for the shower and laundry. Felipe and I shared a strong pot made in the French press. This was usually my favorite twenty minutes of each day, but the dolphins had nudged out the coffee for today's top spot.

The day went on like that: chores, rituals, and enjoying nature's wonders. The cotton ball clouds had left us by sundown, and we were in for a clear, starry night.

As I made my way up onto deck for my night watch, I saw the moon cast a reflection on the water that paved the path we were sailing. A moonlit highway stretched out before us as far as my eyes could see. Over the course of the evening, I saw the Southern Cross moving across the sky.

I had allowed myself to slow down. To go back to a time when our eyes saw so much more than an electronic screen could ever reveal. The stars, the sky, my mind, and *Antares* were somehow magically connected as we glided along over a big ocean toward a very small island.

UNRAVELING

February 23, 2019
Aboard *Antares*
6° 48 south
117° 48 west
Approximately 1,300 miles to Hiva Oa, French Marquesses Islands

Day twenty-one. We were still about 1,300 nautical miles from making landfall at Hiva Oa, in the French Marquesas. We hadn't seen any sign of civilization for twenty-one days. During the last twenty-four hours, light winds had slowed our progress as we averaged only 3.8 knots, and *Antares* pitched and rolled hunting for balance she couldn't find in confused seas. The unsettled motion and light wind caused the sails and rig to bang loudly with each unpredictable pitch of the boat. It was at times, unnerving. At this rate, we would still have another fourteen days in front of us, and I felt like I was starting to unravel a bit.

As social beings, there are always things we tolerate about others. Perhaps it annoys me when someone lingers at my desk too long and I have work to do, or maybe I've turned up the TV too loud and it's annoying my wife. Most of us navigate these situations with manners and patience, in part because we had a good upbringing, and in part because we know that it's only momentary. If I'm at my desk and someone won't leave, I can always excuse myself to use the restroom, or my wife will politely ask me to turn the TV down. When you are confined with the same individuals for a month with very little privacy, trivial things can start to amplify. Small annoyances are easily magnified. They can poison any of the thousand moments when the crew is worn down during a long passage. At times, I struggled to overcome the impulse to scream.

Simon pointed out to me that I always ask where something is before I look for it and that is understandably annoying. Simon and Felipe played music on most days non-stop – it drove me nuts. My character flaw of martyrdom prevented me from speaking out about it often enough. Also, I figured fair was fair since I was outnumbered two to one in favor of the "tunes" (as Simon called them). The fatigue that sets in on a long passage starts to affect mood, and the warning signs are familiar road posts on a well-traveled highway. Outbursts at work fueled by pent up frustration, unnecessary stress, and exhaustion appear in the rearview mirror so fast, like a car about to rear-end you. It was paramount to me that they remained in the rearview mirror.

Holding feelings inside for too long is a recipe for an outburst. They slowly build up over time, and without warning a bale of hay is dropped on the camel's back and it is broken. Then comes the venting and apology, along with the damage to myself and others. This was no way to go through life. I was tired of apologizing to people and the apology seemed less sincere each time it happened.

Something was different that day. First, I recognized the warning signs. *I was getting pissed off.* Second, it dawned on me that I really didn't want to be *that* person anymore. The ocean had stripped away my sense of self-importance. I thought about what to say, along with how and when to say it. After considering their preferences as well as mine, I realized that a suitable compromise was the best solution. As Simon would say, I was "sorting it out". I guess that's why we were out there, to sort things out.

The music had been playing for about five hours, and it was heading toward dinner time. Using the most polite behavior that I could muster, awkwardly I said to them, "Hey guys, can we have a few hours of listening to the wind, the waves, and the canvas?" They graciously nodded. I followed up with, "How about rice and chili for dinner?" They smiled and nodded more enthusiastically. That sure was a lot better than exploding – no apologies, no regrets, no damage. Ironically, after dinner, we listened to music for hours and had a great time.

The lesson had become clear. Part of self-honesty is acknowledging my own feelings. I was learning to speak directly and politely about my preferences, then allowing myself and others a chance to defer and compromise. Simon routinely stated his preferences about anything and everything in his matter-of-fact British accent. I saw in him a role model, a road marker on my journey to honesty. The practice of "Go along to get along" hadn't ended well for me. Upon reflection, it seemed almost cowardly to agree to something while fuming and not saying anything. I don't want to live like a coward or be the guy who snaps and yells, "Turn off that fucking music!" Honest and polite was my new mantra.

On the boat, as in the real world, external forces will push things our way that we may not like. Every time the boat speed dropped, it changed our estimated time of arrival. Seeing the ETA change so drastically was hard on my mind. One day it might show seven days remaining as we clipped along at eight knots. Then, losing the wind, it would suddenly read fourteen days remaining. I would think, "I don't know if I can stand this for another fourteen days." Then, I reminded myself of what I had learned so far: when I am hot, eventually I will be cold; when I am tired, eventually I will sleep; when I am frustrated, eventually it will pass. The lessons I was learning were not only that I had mental, physical, and emotional reserves, but that each moment changes everything. And while I am not in control of everything, I am in control of how I react to everything.

When people learn of my journey, one of the first questions they ask me is, "What was the scariest thing you encountered?" or "What's the biggest storm you were in?" Those questions certainly make sense, and they are likely the same ones that I would have asked only a year ago. Today, I would know to ask, "What did you learn about yourself?" It's hard to tell people in a short conversation that the scariest part of the passage was taking a good, hard, honest look at myself.

THE LAST NIGHT

March 6, 2019
Aboard *Antares*
9° 36 south
138° west
Approaching Hiva Oa, French Marquesses Islands

As we started to wind down the day, our final calculations showed that we should arrive in the Marquesas around 3:00 or 4:00 a.m., and it was the one time we wished we had been going slower. After thirty-three days at sea, it would have been very cool to have that "Land, Ho" moment. That's how you always picture it, right? A clear sunny sky, a fresh breeze, and on the horizon, an island appears on the horizon; someone shouts, "Land, Ho!" The reality of passage making is that you often arrive in the middle of the night which is a bit anti-climactic. The fact that I was very warm, combined with the anticipation of arrival, meant that there would be little to no sleep for me. Since I was going to be wide awake anyway, I offered to take the early watch from 9:00 p.m. to 12:00 a.m., knowing that I would probably stay on deck until 2:00 or 3:00 a.m.

I was straining to see things in the dark for the first time since the Doldrums. The moon, which had been our friend and companion on so much of the journey, had disappeared as she started her new cycle. I'm borrowing Felipe's use of the feminine, because every night he would come on deck to see the moonrise and say, "Hello, moon" and then turn to me and say, "Isn't she beautiful?" Or, sometimes it was a declaration, "She is so beautiful!" Not only was she gone tonight, but the weather, which had been fair for days, had now turned into multiple squall lines which reduced the visibility further. It was a very dark night.

I sat in the cockpit and let the warm, South Pacific trade winds wash over me one last time. I realized that once I was home, some night, unable to sleep, I would stumble out into my living room and think back upon those breezes. I would long for them. Our memory and mind's eye can only hold on to a fraction of the beauty of a place, and photography can only jog the memory. The real experience contains a full spectrum of sight, sound, smell, and touch.

I scanned the horizon in search of lights or shapes in the dark as I tried desperately to see the land we sought. I could see nothing. As we got closer, I felt we should be able to make out the shapes of some of the outlying islands. I began glancing down at the Navionics app on my phone every few minutes, and trying to gauge the distance and angle to where the land should be located. Then, I would peer intensely into the night as if my eyes could pry through the darkness and find the prize we sought.

My mind, tired both from the day and the journey, started to process this reality in the imagination: What if the GPS was off, and we were hundreds of miles away? What if we had missed them and sailed into the great beyond? What if none of this was real? What if, what if, what if... Then, all of a sudden I was startled so greatly I jumped out of my seat – a string of incoming text message alerts went off on my phone! It was all of the texts that had been floating in the air for that last month. I laughed out loud, as I knew then that we were getting close. Soon after, I could make out the looming shape of the mountainous island to my right side, and then what appeared to be a searchlight beam in the sky.

We would still have a few hours to sail, but I was ready for sleep. Simon had come up on deck and relieved me of my watch. Down below, I dropped into my bunk and fell quickly asleep. I was completely exhausted: exhausted from the day, exhausted from the passage, and exhausted from my self-examination over the last nine months. Ready for a break, I was about to arrive in paradise.

My dreams took in all the excitement and sounds of the water against the hull of *Antares* as she effortlessly moved through the water. It was not lost on me as I drifted off to sleep that I would never hear those same sounds again.

SAILING IN, FLYING HOME

After thirty-three days, and 4,100 nautical miles, the weary crew of *Antares* arrived at the marina just outside of Atuona, Hiva Oa, which sits at the base of a majestic mountain. Gazing up, I could only imagine how for ages it has tirelessly caught the clouds that accumulate from the trade winds and held the moisture to sustain life. I would come to find over the next few days that the quiet strength and beauty of the mountain are much like the Marquesans that dwell on this remote island.

I was seeing all of it – life, nature, beauty – as if for the first time. Everything was reaching deeper inside me now that the last layers of fear and ego had been stripped away. I was no longer filtering everything through lenses built to sustain a false reality. I no longer wanted or needed them. A childlike sense of wonder and freedom had taken the place of expectations, perceived wrongs, and the need for perfection or control. The things on my mind were simpler: a soft bed, a good meal, a long shower. I wanted to wander and think, soak it all in, and take as much of it home with me as possible.

We dropped anchor at about 4:30 a.m., had a celebratory beer and fell fast asleep for a few hours. Eager to see the island and get some fresh food, we woke up and set about getting the dinghy in the water. We then re-anchored to a better location inside the breakwater, and gathered up our month-long collection of trash to take ashore.

A taxi drove us downtown, such as it was. This was not a place with chain stores, car dealers or big box retailers; only a few small shops, services, and restaurants. Perhaps they have realized that happiness is not the result of a storage shed full of things they never use. Most local men wore bathing suits, t-shirts, and flip flops, and the women wore shorts and sundresses. I could see no evidence of pretense, and the draw was irresistible. After clearing into customs, we found a quiet spot at a small local restaurant with an amazing view.

I desperately wanted to order everything on the menu that was served on ice, but I limited myself to a cold sparkling water, an orange soda, and an espresso. I worked my way through them while looking out onto one of the most beautiful panoramas I had ever seen. The deep blue ocean suddenly crowded into a small curve in the island, and splashed onto a sandy beach surrounded by palm trees. The towering mountain extended its fingers down to the ocean, showing me how all of it was connected.

Looking east, where the wind and waves originated, it was hard to imagine that *Antares* had carried us so far on our journey. These water highways were here long before us and will be around long after we are gone. It was strange to think we had traveled such a well-worn route. Wind, water, and time the trilogy which shaped that island, continued its work without regard to our brief visit. Contemplating its magnificence reminded me that our own time here is short and insignificant.

The Marquesans seemed like quiet and contented people. They welcomed us with a casual indifference. Unconcerned about our desires and schedules, they took three-hour lunches while children napped on mattresses in the hotel office. We waited impatiently for them to serve us – not a minute early – their schedule would be kept...

It was a ritual they seemed to cherish. Why shouldn't they? We were the ones who were in a hurry. Isn't this the very reason we seek out exotic destinations, so we can slow down? We weren't at a resort in Hawaii where you "relax" between checking emails, and then get upset because the waiter is slow to deliver your Rum Runner cocktail. These islands and their people demanded and deserved our respect. All of this was clear without a word being spoken.

Saying hello to Atuona meant saying goodbye to *Antares*. It was difficult to imagine the next few weeks without Simon's dry wit and Felipe's warm smile. I knew there was a chance we would never see each other again, and the thought saddened me greatly. People often ask me, "Did you get sick of each other?" I always say, "No, we parted while holding back tears." I can't speak for either of them, but I would happily cross another ocean in their company.

As I was about to leave the boat, Simon appeared with a plastic grocery bag tied tightly and said, "Don't open this until you get home." I didn't have to open it to know what was in it; its size, feel, and shape told me that it was a ship's flag. Simon knew that I admired the British Ensign, and that I was a fan of British naval history. The bag contained one of his boat's British Ensigns – something so personal and important to him – I stood there and fought back tears. All I could manage was, "Okay."

Once onshore, I found a taxi that took me to the hotel where we had lunch the day before. At the hotel, I stood in a cold shower for at least thirty minutes, and then I laid down buck-naked on clean sheets while the trade wind breezes blew over my moist body and finally cooled me off.

I spent only a few more nights on Hiva Oa, yet its effect on me would last a lifetime. After that, a small plane flew me fifteen hundred miles further to Tahiti.

Bureaucracy found me in Tahiti, where I struggled with language, culture, and a lack of understanding of how to get my $1,600 French Polynesian travel bond refunded. The banks knew how to sell the bond, but seemed incapable of processing the refund. I vented my frustration to a taxi driver, a Frenchman who had made Tahiti his home in the 1970's. He counseled me in heavily accented French.

"There is no fire in the house."

"I don't understand." I said to him.

"It's the island culture; if it doesn't get done today, it will get done tomorrow."

I let out a hardy laugh and said, "Ok, I understand now."

In that simple phrase, I was reminded of how much I still needed this place, its influence, its indifference, its acceptance. He had told me this because he could see that I was rushing. After a journey that I had been on for nine months, this was the final exam, and I was not being given a passing grade. I still had more to learn.

A few days later, I boarded an Air Tahiti Nui flight home. The flight is a distance nearly identical to the journey we just made – over 4,100 miles – and it would take only eight hours.

Some people ask, "Why bother sailing somewhere that takes you a month when you can fly there in eight hours?" I say in response, that if you drive through a park, you see some grass, trees, and kids playing. If you run through a park, you may also see some animals. If you walk through a park you will see flowers, the bark of the trees, and you will hear the sounds. If you sit in a park you will see, hear, and feel everything – you must sit still. The individual blade of grass, the small bug working so hard, the eyes of the bird above you – it's all there. We rush, and rush, and rush. Our lives are oriented around convenience – fast food drive-through, things to grab and go – quick, quick, quick. What in the world is our hurry? We are only rushing to our own grave. Sailing reminds me to slow down and enjoy the ride.

As Simon had philosophized about why we sailors make these crazy journeys, he had said, "We're dead a long time." Simon is right. We are alive for only a short while, but we are gone for eternity. Dum vivimus vivamus - while we are living, let us live. After thirty years un-lived, and nine months of sorting it out, this lesson would remain my "true north."

There is a risk in sitting still, and perhaps it's the reason most of us don't like to do it very often. In stillness, we hear the voice inside and see the reflection in the pond. Sometimes we don't like what we hear or see. In sitting still, we may discover things about ourselves we didn't know or want to admit. Yet, stillness brings understanding, and understanding is the beginning of truth - at least in this sailor's humble opinion.

The plane home would take me back to a place where all that I had learned would continue to come into focus. In some ways, the real work was still in front of me.

EPILOGUE

When I returned from Polynesia, I started writing this book. It was compiled together from notes that I had taken by hand in my journals as I had wandered across continents, oceans, and islands. While I had learned to slow down and watch sunsets, I found I enjoyed them more after a hard day of work. So, I began to line up work as a captain: charters, deliveries, and sailing instruction.

A few weeks later, I pulled into the tiny parking lot below a famous Shelter Island restaurant named Fiddler's Green, and into a reserved space marked: *Sail San Diego Only.* As I got out of my car, there was a young man locking up the door to the office. I introduced myself. His name was Cal Muir, one of the owners of the company. I told him about my experience, and he said, "Your timing is great, we just had a full-time captain resign." Cal went on to say, "Send me your resume and we'll set up a time to talk." One week later, I was a full-time captain at Sail San Diego.

It was hard for me to imagine how much my life had changed in just one year. After I had left New Horizons, I took advantage of the fact that I was already in Europe to see more of it. Inside of a year, I had gone from Michigan to Corfu Greece, Italy, Switzerland, France, England, Iceland, Michigan, California, Panama, Hiva Oa, Tahiti, and finally to the docks of Sail San Diego. I had spent a year wandering, thinking, contemplating, writing, and envisioning what was next. Suddenly, it had all come together on Shelter Island.

Life settled into a simple routine of work, replenishment, rest, and relaxation. While I had never been good at creating balance in my life, I was starting to figure it out. Having suffered the consequences of a lack of balance, I finally admitted that I was mortal, needed rest, and had a right to express feelings and pursue passions. I finally understood that it was, after all, my life. I had come a long way from that co-dependent childhood.

Long days under the sun were spent as a working captain, taking groups of people out to enjoy the beauty of San Diego and its coast. After we had walked our guests up the gangway, we'd clean and restock our boats, and then have a beer at one of the local watering holes. The only thing left after that was a short walk home and peaceful night's rest.

After a night on the boat, the morning light would make its way into the open companionway of *Trillium*. There is a group of non-native wild parrots in San Diego that start each day with a song of great excitement. I would listen to them singing as I brewed a strong espresso. With my hot coffee in hand, I'd make my way into the cockpit, still moist from the night's dew, and sit peacefully while soaking in the moisture from the air on my sun-tanned skin.

From my boat it was just a short walk along the water to the other side of the island. It was like living in a dream, once only imagined, now real.

There was always a sense of pride as I unlocked the gate at the Sail San Diego docks and walked down the aluminum ramp to the boats. It was hard for me to believe I was one of the four full-time captains at such a highly reputable charter company. There had been many before me and there would be many after me, but that summer, I was part of the crew.

Once on the docks, I would begin to prepare *CrewZen* – the Catalina 400 to which I was assigned – she was my boat. Unplug the boat, unlock the hatch, bring the bean bags up to the bow, unzip the sail bag, ready the lines, bring up the cockpit cushions from below, put out the winch handles, check the beverages, check the engine, turn on the VHF radio, check the safety gear, log the engine hours and fluids, and start hurling friendly jests to the other captains while we waited for the guests to arrive.

The guests would start to anxiously gather at the top of the locked gangway about thirty minutes before the sail. You could tell from fifty feet away that they were eager to sail and excited to meet their captain. The four of us, each on our own boat, would start to position ourselves near the boarding stairway and wait professionally for our guests to be led down by one of the owners or staff members.

It wasn't uncommon for the guests to ask who their captain would be, and we would soon see them looking our way once they found out. Many had been referred by a friend, or perhaps they read about us by name in online reviews. It was an odd feeling to be the object of that kind of mystique and intrigue, but after all, we were what many of them wanted to be. To them, we were free: free of the boardrooms and banquet halls. Yet, I had learned over the last year that freedom wasn't external, it was internal. It was a state of mind.

As we tossed our lines and prepared to leave the docks, we would begin our safety briefing. During these initial few moments, someone would always ask, "How long have you been doing this?" I would usually respond with one of my standard jokes, "I'm a recovering sales executive." I would tell them about the journey I had been on, and about the book I was writing – this book.

Something funny happened as the summer wore on; I noticed that people stopped asking the question. Externally, everything I was doing was exactly the same as it had been on day one: untie the boat, ease her out of the slip, trade a few barbs and jokes with the other captains – none of that had changed. So, I wondered, what changed? Why was it that no one ever asked the question anymore? Then it dawned on me: people weren't asking because at some point, what they saw me do seemed natural and effortless. Another milestone in my life had passed as quietly as an ebbing tide.

Every charter was different. Sometimes it would be a private charter for a company, family, or a group of friends on an annual vacation. Other times it was a mix of unrelated individuals and families. Many times, you couldn't tell the difference until you started asking questions. Within minutes of boarding a boat, strangers often become fast friends. It all happened right in front of my eyes.

There were moments when the boat was filled with excitement during a "Sail Before the Veil" bridal shower. Sometimes it was mourning the loss of a loved one during a burial at sea. I was always hugging people – mostly in joy, occasionally in sadness. I must have told the same jokes and stories a few hundred times to endless smiles and laughter. I held the helm steady while a young man got down on his knee and proposed marriage to his girlfriend, and I held a man as he cried after pouring his beloved mother's ashes into the sea.

On most days, we went out beyond Point Loma, which for some people was the first time they had been on the ocean. It's hard to describe the kind of joy you feel when you're taking someone on the ocean for the first time. When we were lucky, our trip was graced by a whale, dolphins or pelicans flying so low and so close that you could look into their eyes.

Then, the sun would begin to set as we sailed back toward Point Loma and finally took up station at the entrance to America's Cup Harbor. Everyone suddenly stopped chatting and just watched it melt into the hill above the harbor; for a few moments, they just released sounds expressing amazement. We had transported them from their busy lives to a moment in time that they would always remember. I was their captain for that moment. It was the summer of a lifetime.

Ultimately, I had done what I had set out to do, and in so doing, I had made a change in my life that was long overdue. But in the end, it wasn't the external change that mattered, it was the internal change. The lessons I learned will be part of the instruments that I use to determine my course in life. I am the captain. I am navigating honestly and with open eyes.

Life is much like the ocean. A rising tide lifts our boat. Low tide exposes things below the surface we may wish would remain hidden. There are days on end of nothing but calm, and then suddenly, storms appear on the horizon. A wave from nowhere can knock you down. We can set a course with determination, or we can simply drift. In both cases we end up somewhere.

I hope that in this book you have found some inspiration for your own journey and some cautionary tales from mine.

I wish you fair winds and following seas,
Captain Cam

Thank You!

Your support made this journey possible:

Sail San Diego - the owners, captains, and staff

GLC Training - Captain Mel

My second family in Michigan: Dave, Morgan, Miles, and Porter

The "crew" on Clinton River - Susie, Capt. Ron, Capt. Coll, Jeff

New Horizons - Fred, Rob, Bart, Berith, and Julie

Antares - Simon and Felipe

Laury Falter - thank you for your endless encouragement to write!

Joe Monahan - for teaching me, "every word matters."

My Brother - for raising me and fostering my love of sailing and the ocean.

Laurie, Brian and Christie - thank you for putting up with my endless eccentricities and adventures in this life.

ABOUT THE AUTHOR

Cam spent a memorable part of his youth in Dana Point, California. He attributes his love of the water to those formative teen years wandering around the harbor. He also muses about the role of genetics in his passion, coming from ten-generations of fishermen on his mother's side in Ireland.

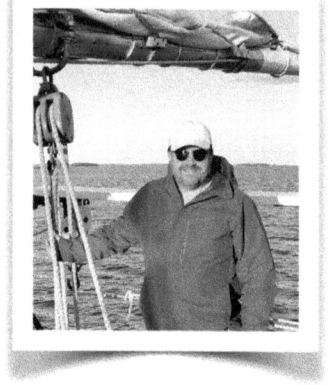

After building a successful career in sales and leadership, he took a two-year sabbatical to rearrange his life to what he considered to be "more-perfect priorities".

Cam learned to sail in 1983 at a U.S. Navy recreational sailing program while serving in the United States Marines. Since then, he has sailed all over the United States, the Mediterranean, and the South Pacific. He is a licensed captain and Sailing Instructor.

He resides in Southern California, with his wife and their two dogs, where he continues to work on his first fictional book The Captain. He can be found on most weekends on his boat off the coast of San Diego.

www.ingramcontent.com/pod-product-compliance
Lightning Source LLC
Chambersburg PA
CBHW070206060426
42445CB00033B/1650